Financial Analysis with an Electronic Calculator

Fourth Edition

Mark A. White
University of Virginia

Irwin
McGraw-Hill

Boston   Burr Ridge, IL   Dubuque, IA   Madison, WI   New York   San Francisco   St. Louis
Bangkok   Bogotá   Caracas   Lisbon   London   Madrid
Mexico City   Milan   New Delhi   Seoul   Singapore   Sydney   Taipei   Toronto

McGraw-Hill Higher Education

A Division of The McGraw·Hill Companies

2 3 4 5 6 7 8 9 0 BKM/BKM 9 0 9 8 7 6 5 4 3 2 1 0

ISBN 0-07-229973-8

http://www.mhhe.com

PREFACE TO THE FOURTH EDITION

Rapidly changing information and communication technologies have had an enormous impact on the financial world. Today's fast-moving markets place a premium on "running the numbers" swiftly and accurately. Financial calculators are affordable and easy-to-learn tools for accomplishing both of these objectives.

The purpose of this book is to provide information and procedures enabling students to master their financial calculators while simultaneously gaining a deeper understanding of financial mathematics. It is designed to be used as a self-contained supplement in the introductory financial management course. Complete instructions are included for solving all major problem types on three common models of financial calculator – Hewlett Packard's HP-10B, Sharp Electronics' EL-733A and Texas Instruments' BA II Plus. The fourth edition contains 40 updated problems drawn from several of the leading introductory finance texts.

This book owes a tremendous debt to the hundreds of finance students I've had the pleasure of teaching at the University over the past ten years. I am grateful to my good friend and finance colleague, Janet Todd, for her careful reading of this revised edition and to Michele Janicek at Irwin/McGraw-Hill for her unflagging assistance in bringing this project to fruition. I dedicate this book to my beautiful wife, Susie, and our two exceptional children, Katie and Skye.

Mark A. White

Mark A. White
University of Virginia
Charlottesville, Virginia
July 1999

ABOUT THE AUTHOR

Mark White is an Associate Professor at the University of Virginia's McIntire School of Commerce, where he teaches finance. Prior to receiving PhD and MBA degrees in Finance from Michigan State University, he earned an MS in Ecology from Michigan State and a BA in Biology from Kalamazoo College. His research interests center on the use of valuation models in finance and the impact of environmental issues on corporate strategy and firm performance.

TABLE OF CONTENTS

3. Valuation of Financial Instruments

4. Using the Cash Flow Registers

5. Statistics

6. Additional Problems

Chapter One

INTRODUCTION

"But the age of chivalry is gone. That of sophisters, economists and calculators has succeeded ..."

— Edmund Burke

Financial calculators are a relatively recent yet widespread addition to modern finance. By providing students with greater speed and accuracy in problem-solving, they can, if used correctly, greatly enhance the learning process. Mastering the field of finance requires practice and often repetitious computation. Financial calculators can eliminate the tedium associated with these calculations and allow you to better focus on the overall analysis. Furthermore, financial calculators allow instructors to introduce more relevant "real world" examples without fear of overwhelming students with numerical details. Indeed, the dependence of the financial industry on calculating machines of all types – financial calculators, personal computers, and mainframes – might lead you to wonder how the financial world got along without these 'electronic brains' in the first place.

Suffice it to say that finance has benefited tremendously from advances in electronic technology. The pocket calculators of today run faster, contain more memory and are hardwired to perform far more advanced calculations than Philadelphia's legendary ENIAC computer.[1] Tables of so-called interest rate 'factors,' designed to ease calculations by presenting the results of various combinations of time periods and interest rates, are well on their way to becoming a thing of the past. Financial calculators can provide more accurate solutions to a greater universe of problems than is possible by using tables alone. Some problems requiring iterative solutions are practically impossible to solve without electronic means. You can, of course, use a financial calculator to derive all the factors found in the various Present Value/Future Value tables.

For all of this, calculators pose hidden dangers for beginning students. They are not and can not be substitutes for clear-headed analysis. Far too many individuals tend to treat financial calculators as "black boxes" that provide answers to those initiates fortunate enough to press the secret key sequences. Calculators are a means, not an end. According to the author of a popular finance textbook,

---

[1]The Electronic Numerical Integrator and Calculator (ENIAC) is widely regarded as the first successful high-speed electronic digital computer. Developed by John Eckert and John Mauchly at the University of Pennsylvania, it was completed in 1946. The computer used over 18,000 vacuum tubes, stood two stories high and occupied 1,500 square feet of floor space. It required so much electricity that surrounding city lights dimmed when it was running.

1

"If finance was merely calculating numbers, taking a finance course and reading this text would be a waste! All you would have to do is purchase a good quality financial calculator, read its owners manual, and start making financial decisions. As you progress through this text you will see that the proper setup of the problem is the difficult part. Once this step is accomplished, the calculations are easily done ..."[2]

Learning finance requires dedication and a willingness to try to understand the *relationships* among various financial variables. Financial calculators can assist in this process but mere possession of one does not confer instant knowledge.[3] Ownership of a financial calculator is not a license to stop thinking!

Calculators vs. Computers

The use of a calculator to solve financial problems is frequently disparaged in favor of computers running analytical software. There is no doubt that personal (and larger) computers are capable of analyzing much more complex situations than you might wish to tackle on a pocket calculator. On the other hand, the vast majority of problems encountered in the classroom are generally quite simple. Financial calculators require a much smaller investment in capital and training time, as compared with personal computers. Thus, they are likely to be used in greater numbers than personal computers.

Different situations require different tools. In some cases, only paper and pencil are necessary to reach a "ballpark" figure. In others, the greater accuracy afforded by a financial calculator is appropriate. More complicated analyses may require a personal computer, and even greater levels of sophistication may call for the use of a mainframe or supercomputer. Similar circumstances are found in other fields. Consider, for instance, the different types of saws used in building a house. Financial calculators might be likened to the handsaw, a versatile tool that performs many jobs. Personal computers, with their greater bulk and greater capabilities, are akin to a Skilsaw™ or portable circular saw. Finally, mainframe computers share many features with tablesaws (permanent mounting, optimized for fast processing of large jobs, etc). The point is that different tools are used to solve different problems, and that the most powerful tool is not always the most appropriate one.

---

[2]Ramesh K. S. Rao, *Fundamentals of Financial Management*. (New York: Macmillan Publishing Co., 1989), 808 pp.

[3]The author has first-hand acquaintance with a number of students who bought an electronic calculator the night before their first exam, apparently expecting the mysteries of the financial universe to be revealed at the appropriate time. The results were (predictably) dismal.

Calculator Models Covered in this Book

Three models of financial calculator are discussed in this book: Hewlett-Packard's HP-10B, Sharp Electronics' EL-733A and Texas Instruments' BA II Plus. These calculators are the most common models found in the introductory finance course. They possess roughly the same set of features and sell for approximately the same price (Table 1-1).

Table 1-1. Comparative Features of Financial Calculators

Feature	Hewlett-Packard HP-10B	Sharp Electronics EL-733A	Texas Instruments BA II Plus
Arithmetic Functions	yes	yes	yes
Time Value of Money	yes	yes	yes
Data Entry Format	algebraic	algebraic	algebraic
Memory	yes	yes	yes
Multiple compounding	yes		yes
Interest Rate Conversions	yes	yes	yes
Loan Amortization	yes	yes	yes
Cash Flow Analysis	yes	yes	yes
Bond Pricing			yes
Depreciation			yes
Break-Even Analysis			yes
Descriptive Statistics	yes	yes	yes
Weighted Averages	yes		
Regression Analysis	yes	yes	yes
Percentage Change	yes	yes	yes
Margin/Markup	yes	yes	yes
Date Functions			yes
Trigonometric Functions			yes
Suggested Retail Price	$50	$46	$45

More advanced calculators are also available and in many cases a good investment, particularly if a student intends to pursue further studies in finance. Many of the techniques and problem-solving methods discussed in this book apply equally well to other models by the same manufacturer.

Hewlett-Packard HP-10B

Hewlett-Packard's HP-10B is in some ways the successor to the firm's venerable HP-12C, which was first introduced in 1981. It is an entry-level calculator offering a surprisingly complete array of features, including the ability to analyze uneven streams of cash flows. Potential users put off by Hewlett-Packard's traditional use of "Reverse Polish Notation"[4] or RPN logic in its calculators will appreciate the switch to an algebraic mode of entry. The HP-10B is a finely made, dependable calculator that provides easy access to a wide array of financial functions.

Sharp Electronics EL-733A

In 1992, Sharp Electronics introduced the EL-733A, a slightly modified version of its popular EL-733 financial calculator. The two models are functionally equivalent, but the larger keys on the EL-733A make it much easier to use. Its features are nearly identical to the HP-10B, although it can be often be found at a slightly lower price. The EL-733A has an interesting display designed to increase its acceptance in international circles. Instead of the comma (,) normally used to designate multiples of 1,000, the EL-733A uses an apostrophe (').

Texas Instruments BA II Plus

The BA II Plus, released in 1991, is the latest incarnation of Texas Instruments' original Business Analyst calculator. It boasts more features than either of the other two models covered in this book, and uses a unique system of menus for data entry and problem solution. It is priced similarly to the HP-10B.

Notation

The following conventions are used to identify key sequences:

- *Numerical entries* are shown without modification, e.g., 23.00

- *Primary keys* have a physical location and appear in boxes, e.g., PMT

---

[4]The term "Reverse Polish Notation" honors its developer, the Polish logician Jan Lukasiewicz (1878-1956). Hewlett-Packard's implementation differs from Lukasiewicz' original notation, which placed the operators *before* the numbers or variables. Hewlett-Packard calculators require the operators be entered *after* the variables, hence, 'reverse' polish notation.

- *Secondary keys* are enclosed within curly braces, e.g., {NPV}.
  Pressing a modifier key, e.g., ⌐2nd⌐, invokes the secondary function
  generally printed slightly above the physical key location.[5]

Incidentally, this book is not intended as a substitute for the operating manual that came with your financial calculator. Its goal is to show how a financial calculator can assist you in learning the techniques of *financial analysis*, not reiterate the specifics of each and every key on each and every calculator. Margin/markup functions are not included because they are fairly uncommon in the introductory finance course. Several useful features peculiar to the BA II Plus, e.g., depreciation, advanced bond pricing, dates and trigonometric functions, have also been left out for reasons of space and because they are only hardwired into one of the three calculators discussed in this book. What's left is a series of examples carefully chosen to reflect the types of problems you are likely to meet in an introductory finance course. Your mastery of this tool will be rewarded by a deeper understanding of finance and (possibly!) higher grades.

Housekeeping Functions

Before solving financial problems, it's best to familiarize yourself with the basic housekeeping functions, e.g., clearing memory registers, setting display formats, and determining the compounding and payment modes. These are explained in the following paragraphs.

Memory Registers

All calculators have areas of memory, called registers, where variables and intermediate results of calculations are stored. There are essentially three groups of registers: 1) Display registers, 2) Financial registers and 3) Data registers. As their name suggests, display registers are used to display data. The financial registers are used to solve problems involving the time value of money (TVM) and are sometimes known as the TVM registers. Depending on the problem type, data registers may hold intermediate results of computations, statistical data or cash flow information.

It is extremely important to CLEAR or "zero out" the requisite memory registers before beginning a new calculation.[6] Most errors, particularly in time value of money problems, are due to a failure to clear the appropriate memory registers. Registers can be cleared individually, as a group, or all at once. Table 1-2 identifies the sets of registers peculiar to different calculator models and the keystrokes necessary for clearing them.

---

[5]The HP-10B's modifier key is a large orange square. It appears in this book as ☐.

[6]Some memory registers can be "cleared" by storing zeros in them.

Table 1-2. Clearing Entries and Memory Registers

Function	Hewlett-Packard HP-10B	Sharp Electronics EL-733A	Texas Instruments BA II Plus
Clear last digit	`←`	`→`	`→`
Clear display	`C`	`C·CE`	`C/CE`
Clear error messages	`←` or `C`	`C·CE`	`C/CE`
Clear M(emory) registers	`☐`{CLEAR ALL}	0 `X→M`	`2nd` {MEM} `2nd` {CLR Work}
Clear Markup registers	`☐`{CLEAR ALL}	`2ndF` {CA}	`2nd` {CLR Work}
Clear TVM registers	`☐`{CLEAR ALL}	`2ndF` {CA}	`2nd` {CLR TVM}
Clear Cash Flow registers	`☐`{CLEAR ALL}	`2ndF` {CA}	`2nd` {CLR Work}
Clear Statistical registers	`☐`{CLΣ}	`2ndF` {CA}	`2nd` {CLR Work}
Delete statistical data	`☐`{Σ−}	`CD`	`2nd` {DEL}
Clear all registers	`☐`{CLEAR ALL}	`2ndF` {CA}*	`2nd` {QUIT}**
Quit worksheet mode	n/a	n/a	`2nd` {QUIT}
Reset default modes	***	n/a	`2nd` {Reset} `ENTER`

* This key sequence does NOT clear the **M**(emory) register; even turning the calculator on and off won't do that. Clear the **M** register by pressing 0 `X→M` or `RM` `+/−` `M+`

** This sequence only works in standard calculator mode. Use `2nd` {CLR Work} to clear a specific worksheet before returning to standard calculator mode.

*** To reset all calculator modes, press and hold the `C` key, then simultaneously press and hold down the `N` and `Σ+` keys at each end of the top row. Releasing all three should display 'ALL CLr' and reset the calculator's internal defaults.

Display Formats

The HP-10B and BA II Plus provide an option for displaying numbers in either US or European formats.[7] Press ☐ {./,} to toggle between these formats on Hewlett Packard's HP-10B. On the BA II Plus, press [2nd] {Format} and select the 'EUR' separator format by pressing [2nd] {SET} once you've scrolled to the decimal separator section of the format worksheet.

Setting the display to a fixed number of decimal places makes it easier to enter data and to read results. Two decimal places are most commonly used, although you may display other numbers of fixed digits by substituting a different number (from 0 to 9) in place of the '2' shown below. Answers will be rounded to conform to the desired number of displayed digits, although all digits are retained when performing internal calculations. Very large numbers are displayed using scientific notation. To set the display format to *two* decimal places, use the following key sequences:[8]

- HP-10B: ☐ {DISP} 2

- EL-733A: [2ndF] {TAB} 2

- BA II Plus: [2nd] {Format} 2 [ENTER]

Use the following keystrokes to reset displays to all possible decimal places (floating point format):

- HP-10B: ☐ {DISP} [.]

- EL-733A: [2ndF] {TAB} [.]

- BA II Plus: [2nd] {Format} 9 [ENTER]

Sign Changes

Financial transactions often consist of an initial cash flow followed by subsequent cash flows of opposite sign. For instance, a bank might make a loan to an individual (a *cash outflow*) expecting to receive a series of loan payments (*cash inflows*) in the future. From the borrower's perspective, he/she receives an initial sum of money (a cash inflow) by agreeing to repay the loan according to some schedule (cash outflows). Sign changes are used to identify the direction of these

---

[7]In the United States, decimal points are indicated by periods and commas are used as digit separators. In Europe, the situation is reversed. Hence, 1,958,000.00 (US) = 1.958.000,00 (European). The BA II Plus can also display *dates* in either US or European formats, i.e., month first versus date first. These options are changed in the Format worksheets.

[8]Some instructors recommend *four* decimal places for increased accuracy. It's always a good idea to use four decimal places when working with interest rates.

cash flows. Cash outflows are entered as negative numbers and cash inflows are entered as positive numbers. To enter a negative number on any of the calculators discussed in this book, first press the appropriate digit keys and *then press the change sign key*, $\boxed{+/-}$. Do **NOT** use the minus sign key, $\boxed{-}$, as its effects are quite unpredictable.

Annuities and Annuities Due

In finance, timing is everything. It makes a difference whether monies are paid at the beginning or end of a period. *Ordinary* annuities assume payment is made at the *end* of a period. *Annuities due* assume payment is made at the *beginning* of a period. In general, most problems (in the classroom and in real life) assume payment is made at the end of a period. During the introductory course it is probably best not to even use the annuity due feature, as you may forget to reset the calculator for subsequent problems. Moreover, all annuity due problems can be solved using techniques applicable to ordinary annuities. However, for those who must, use the following keystrokes to adjust for payments occurring at the beginning of a period:

- HP-10B: $\boxed{}$ {BEG / END}

- EL-733A: $\boxed{BGN}$

- BA II Plus: $\boxed{2nd}$ {BGN} $\boxed{2nd}$ {SET} $\boxed{2nd}$ {QUIT}

In all cases, these keystrokes act as toggles, i.e., pressing the same sequence again returns you to ordinary annuity or "END" mode.

Compounding Frequency

One last issue that must be dealt with is the compounding frequency per period. For both pedagogical and practical reasons, most problems in the introductory finance course assume compounding occurs **once** per period. Although there are a few exceptions (semiannual bonds are a notable example), it is often more confusing to switch between different compounding frequencies, i.e., daily, monthly, quarterly and semiannually than it is to simply leave your calculator set to compound interest once per period.

Sharp's EL-733A provides users no choice – all time value of money and cash flow computations assume a compounding frequency of once per period. Hewlett-Packard's HP-10B and Texas Instruments' BA II Plus allow you to set different compounding periods. Unfortunately for beginning students, *the default mode on each of these calculators is twelve times per period (monthly)*. Therefore, it is very important that users of these models know how to determine and change the compounding frequency. Both models allegedly 'remember' the most recent setting, even after the power has been turned off. Experience has shown, however, that these settings can sometimes be changed bouncing around in a backpack or purse.

To check the setting for compounding frequency on the HP-10B, press the ☐ key, then press and briefly hold the ⌑INPUT⌑ key. This performs two valuable functions; it clears the Time Value of Money registers *and* displays the compounding frequency. The default frequency is 12 times per period, displayed as "12 P_Yr". To change it, enter the desired compounding frequency, e.g., 1, then press ☐ {P/YR}. It's best to confirm that this has occurred before beginning any lengthy calculations.

You can specify both payment frequency *and* compounding frequency on the BA II Plus. Problems involving a discrepancy between the two are rare in the introductory finance curriculum, and payment frequency and compounding frequency should normally be set to the same number. To set both to once per period, first press ⌑2nd⌑ {P/Y} 1 ⌑ENTER⌑, then press ⌑↓⌑ 1 ⌑ENTER⌑ (to set the compounding frequency). Pressing ⌑2nd⌑ {QUIT} returns you to standard calculator mode.

Set comp period (handwritten margin note)

One last word on compounding frequency – as noted previously, most calculator errors arise from a failure to properly clear the memory registers. On the HP-10B and BA II Plus, incorrect compounding regimes run a close second.

Troubleshooting

If despite all your best efforts you can't get the correct answer, or the dreaded "Error" message appears, quickly run through the following checklist:

1. Did you CLEAR all the registers?

2. Is the compounding frequency set to one time per year?
   [HP-10B and BA-II Plus only]

3. Is the calculator in END mode?

4. Did you enter negative numbers using the ⌑+/−⌑ key?

If the answer is "No" to any of these questions, clear and reset your calculator and try again. Other possible sources of error include neglecting to make one set of cash flows negative and one set of cash flows positive when solving for an unknown interest rate or number of periods, and on the EL-733A, forgetting in which mode (Standard, Financial or Statistics) the calculator is set.

Chapter Two

THE TIME VALUE OF MONEY

"I will gladly pay you Tuesday for a hamburger today."

– Wimpy

According to economists, most people display *positive time preference* with regard to decisions about money. Given a choice, individuals would rather receive a dollar (or pound or Deutschemark or ringgit or whatever) sooner rather than later. Thus, we say that money has "time value" – a dollar to be paid in the future is not worth as much as a dollar paid now. This is because a dollar received in the present can be invested to earn interest. Suppose, for instance, you wished to have $100 in your bank account at the end of this year. Because your bank pays interest, you need to deposit some lesser amount today. The interest you earn over the next year makes up the difference between your initial deposit (*present value*) and the final amount (*future value*). Financial mathematics deals with relationships between Present Value, Future Value, Payment, Interest Rate and Time. If you know any three of these variables, it's possible to solve for a fourth.[1] Although the basic equations governing transformations between present money and future money have been known for literally thousands of years,[2] the advent of the electronic calculator has alleviated much of the tedium and imprecision associated with former methods. This chapter provides an introduction to basic problem-solving using the time value of money (TVM) registers on a financial calculator.

How To Solve Financial Problems

Beginning finance students sometimes freeze up upon learning that they will be expected to solve so-called "story problems." High school memories of trying to determine where to bury the survivors from a train wreck involving two trains traveling at x miles per hour for y hours and meeting at point z can cause a relapse of *terror mathematicus*.[3] Fortunately, there are a few "tricks" you can employ to get a handle on most financial story problems. The first involves drawing a time line, or cash flow diagram.

---

[1] Two of the four variables involved in a particular calculation must be Interest Rate and Time. Sometimes it is possible to solve for a fifth variable (if one knows the other four).

[2] Aristotle (384 - 322 BC) condemned the charging of interest as an evil practice.

[3] As Foster Leghorn might say, "It's a joke, son ... you don't bury *survivors*."

Cash Flow Diagrams

Cash flow diagrams are useful analytical tools because they allow you to determine at a glance whether money is coming or going and at which points in time (Figure 2-1).

Figure 2-1. A Cash Flow Diagram

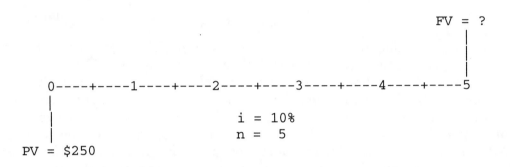

A few observations about cash flow diagrams are in order. They are usually drawn beginning at t=0, your present position in time. Cash outflows are indicated by vertical lines going down, while cash inflows are shown as vertical lines going up. It is good practice to label the axis and to note the interest rate prevailing over the period in question. Unknowns are indicated by variable names and sometimes by question marks. *Compounding* is the process of moving cash flows forward in time; *discounting* refers to movements backward in time. In Figure 2-1, a cash outflow of $250, perhaps in the form of a bank deposit, is made *today* and an unspecified cash inflow resulting from the compounding process is expected 5 periods in the future. Interest accrues at the rate of 10 percent per period.

Identifying Variables and Writing Equations

The second step in solving a financial problem is to identify the known and unknown variables and to write the appropriate equations. If the cash flow diagram has been drawn correctly, this should be a fairly simple exercise, for it is usually apparent which variables are known and which must be solved for.

The explanation and derivation of the time value of money equations is beyond the scope of this book, but is a significant part of most introductory financial management textbooks.[4] There are four basic relationships:

---

[4]Many good references can be found in the bibliography.

$$FV = PV \times (1 + i)^n \tag{1}$$

$$PV = \frac{FV}{(1 + i)^n} \tag{2}$$

$$FV = PMT \cdot \left[\frac{(1 + i)^n - 1}{i} \right] \tag{3}$$

$$PV = PMT \cdot \left[\frac{1 - \dfrac{1}{(1 + i)^n}}{i} \right] \tag{4}$$

where:

FV	=	future value
PV	=	present value
PMT	=	payment
i	=	interest rate per period
n	=	number of periods

Your financial calculator is hardwired to solve for any variable in each of these equations if the other three variables are provided as input. The calculators discussed in this book can also solve a fifth equation:

$$PV = PMT \cdot \left[\frac{1 - \dfrac{1}{(1 + i)^n}}{i} \right] + \frac{FV}{(1 + i)^n} \tag{5}$$

Equation 5, better known as the "bond equation," contains all five TVM variables and is a simple combination of Equations 2 and 4.

Present Value / Future Value Tables

Before electronic calculators became widely available, tables of interest rate "factors" were state-of-the-art in financial problem-solving. Old habits change slowly, and some instructors still insist students perform calculations with nothing more than paper, pencil and these tables. Even though most readers of this book will be using a financial calculator, it is still useful to know how to solve problems using the Present Value/Future Value tables.

Interest rate factors are shorthand expressions for the complex terms of Equations 1 through 4. Thus,

$$\text{FVIF}_{(i\%, n)} = \text{"Future Value Interest Factor"} = (1 + i)^n$$

$$\text{PVIF}_{(i\%, n)} = \text{"Present Value Interest Factor"} = \frac{1}{(1 + i)^n}$$

$$\text{FVAF}_{(i\%, n)} = \text{"Future Value Annuity Factor"} = \left[\frac{(1 + i)^n - 1}{i}\right]$$

and
$$\text{PVAF}_{(i\%, n)} = \text{"Present Value Annuity Factor"} = \left[\frac{1 - \dfrac{1}{(1 + i)^n}}{i}\right]$$

Equations 1 through 5 can therefore be re-written:

$$\text{FV} = \text{PV} \cdot \text{FVIF}_{(i\%,\ n)} \tag{1'}$$

$$\text{PV} = \text{FV} \cdot \text{PVIF}_{(i\%,\ n)} \tag{2'}$$

$$\text{FV} = \text{PMT} \cdot \text{FVAF}_{(i\%,\ n)} \tag{3'}$$

$$\text{PV} = \text{PMT} \cdot \text{PVAF}_{(i\%,\ n)} \tag{4'}$$

$$\text{PV} = \text{PMT} \cdot \text{PVAF}_{(i\%,\ n)} + \text{FV} \cdot \text{PVIF}_{(i\%,\ n)} \tag{5'}$$

Equations 1' through 5' provide a handy method for summarizing information to be entered in a financial calculator's TVM registers. Consider Equation 3' – if FV, i and n are known, then we must be solving for PMT.

The Present Value/Future Value tables are not in themselves great mysteries. They contain frequently used combinations of time and interest rates. But if your needs are not in the tables, say 7 and 1/2 percent interest for 13 years, you'll have to make a "best guess," which is subject to error. Financial calculators improve accuracy and make it easier to solve for certain variables, e.g., time.

To show the relationship between the Present Value/Future Value tables and a calculator's hardwired TVM functions, use the calculator to replicate the tables. They all assume values of $1 for the Present Value, Future Value or Payment, so you need only enter '1' into the appropriate register and key in the corresponding interest rate and time period. Examples 2-1 and 2-2 provide practice in doing this.[5]

---

[5]Check to make sure the compounding frequency is set to once per period and CLEAR ALL REGISTERS before beginning a new problem!

2-1) Determine the Present Value Interest Factor (PVIF) for ten periods at 8 percent.

HP-10B	EL-733A	BA II Plus
1.0000 FV	1.0000 FV	1.0000 FV
10.0000 N	10.0000 n	10.0000 N
8.0000 I/YR	8.0000 i	8.0000 I/Y
PV -0.4632	COMP PV -0.4632	CPT PV -0.4632

$PVIF_{(8\%, \, 10)} = 0.4632$

2-2) What is the Future Value Annuity Factor (FVAF) of 6.5 percent for nine periods?

HP-10B	EL-733A	BA II Plus
1.000 PMT	1.000 PMT	1.000 PMT
9.000 N	9.000 n	9.000 N
6.500 I/YR	6.500 i	6.500 I/Y
FV -11.732	COMP FV -11.732	CPT FV -11.732

$FVAF_{(6.5\%, \, 9)} = 11.732$

Before checking these answers against the Present Value/Future Value Tables in Appendix B, let's see if they agree with our intuition. In Example 2-1, we know that PV is always less than FV, due to the Time Value of Money. Since FV = $1, PV must be something less, in this case $0.4632, which corresponds to the PVIF factor at 8% for 10 periods (Appendix B.2). In Example 2-2, we know that the FV of the annuity must be at least 9, because that would be true at an interest rate of zero percent. An FVAF of 11.732 seems reasonable, and indeed lies between the FVAF factors for 6 percent and 7 percent shown in Appendix B. By the way, the answers appear as *negative* numbers because the present value is *positive*. Entering a negative present value produces a positive future value.

Future Value of a Present Sum

In a "future value" problem, you're trying to determine an amount of money at some period in the future based upon a known sum at t=0. Note that t=0 does not necessarily mean *today*. For instance, Example 2-3 is a popular way of illustrating the impact of compound interest:

2-3) In 1626, Peter Minuit supposedly purchased Manhattan Island from the Canarsee Indians for 60 guilders, or about $24. Suppose the Indians had invested their proceeds from the sale at a 5 percent annual interest rate. How much would they have accumulated by 1998, 372 years later?

Step 1. *Construct a cash flow diagram indicating the direction of each cash flow and the known and unknown variables.*

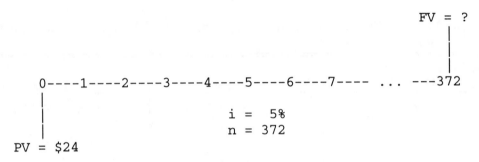

Step 2. *Write the appropriate equation describing this problem.*

$$FV = \$24\,(1+.05)^{372} \quad \textbf{or} \quad FV = \$24 \cdot FVIF_{(5\%,\,372)}$$

Step 3. *Enter the data into the proper registers – but be sure to CLEAR them first and change signs where necessary!*

HP-10B	EL-733A	BA II Plus
-24 PV	-24 PV	-24 PV
372 N	372 n	372 N
5 I/YR	5 i	5 I/Y
FV ≈ $1.83 billion	COMP FV ≈ $1.83 billion	CPT FV ≈ $1.83 billion

At an annual interest rate of 5 percent, the future value of $24 compounded for 372 years = $1,830,756,125 or about $1.83 billion. At 10 percent, it equals 6.0019×10^{16} or about 60 quadrillion dollars!

In this case, t=0 refers to the year 1626. The original payment of $24 represents a cash outflow (deposit) from the Indians' point of view and is entered as a negative number. The $1.83 billion is what the Canarsee would have hypothetically received 372 years in the future. Of course, one could also diagram this problem from the bank's point of view, treating the $24 deposit as a cash inflow and the accrued interest and principal as a cash outflow. (Try it! If the $24 initial deposit is positive, the FV will be negative).

Present Value of a Future Sum

Present value problems are concerned with how much money you need now in order to achieve some goal in the future. They bear a strong relationship to future value problems, and you've probably already noticed that Equations 1 and 2 are simple rearrangements of one another and that the PVIF and FVIF factors are reciprocals. Example 2-4 illustrates a typical present value problem and the steps in its solution.

2-4) Grandfather White is very proud of his new granddaughter, Katie. He's figured out that she will need approximately $100,000 to attend college when she's eighteen, and he would like to give her a gift to ensure she achieves this goal. Ignoring taxes and inflation and assuming Katie will be able to earn a constant 6 percent interest rate over the next 18 years, how much money should Grandfather White give to Katie *now*?

Step 1. Construct a cash flow diagram

```
                                                    FV = $100,000
                                                        |
                                                        |
                                                        |
    0----1----2----3----4----5----6----7-- ... --18
    |
    |                           i =  6%
    |                           n = 18
PV = ?
```

Step 2. Write the appropriate equation

$$PV = \frac{\$100,000}{(1+.06)^{18}} \quad \textbf{or} \quad PV = \$100,000 \cdot PVIF_{(6\%,\ 18)}$$

(example continued on next page)

17

Step 3. Enter the data into the appropriate registers

HP-10B	EL-733A	BA II Plus
100,000 [FV]	100'000 [FV]	100,000 [FV]
18 [N]	18 [n]	18 [N]
6 [I/YR]	6 [i]	6 [I/Y]
[PV] -35,034	[COMP] [PV] -35'034	[CPT] [PV] -35,034

Grandfather White should write a check for $35,034 to ensure Katie will have the $100,000 necessary to attend college in 18 years.

If you are just beginning to use your calculator, you might want to check the calculator's solution against the Present Value/Future Value tables to make sure you're on the right track. (It's also useful to know how to use the tables in case your calculator suddenly goes dead in the middle of a test!) According to Appendix B, the PVIF at 6 percent for 18 years equals 0.3503. Multiplying this figure by $100,000 equals $35,030. The difference between this answer and the calculator's is due to rounding error.

Future Value of an Ordinary Annuity

Solving for the future value of an ordinary annuity allows you to determine how much money has accumulated as the result of a series of periodic payments. The term annuity has a very special meaning in finance – it refers to a series of *equal* payments, *equally* spaced, occurring *every* period. As mentioned earlier, ordinary annuities assume payment occurs at the end of a period, while annuities due assume payment takes place at the beginning. Unless specifically told otherwise, assume all payments occur at the end of given period (and be certain your calculator is set to reflect this – see Chapter One).

2-5) Fourteen-year old Skye is crazy about cars and is determined to buy one as soon as he gets his drivers' license on his 16th birthday. He's just taken a job that will allow him to save $50 per month for the next 24 months. His money is deposited in the Earlysville State Bank earning 6 percent annual interest, compounded monthly (i = 0.5 percent per month). How much money will he have in the account when he turns 16?

Step 1.   Construct a cash flow diagram

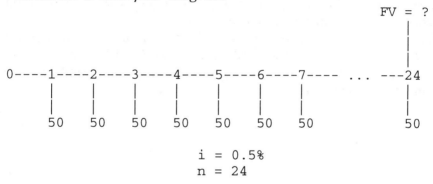

$$i = 0.5\%$$
$$n = 24$$

Step 2.   Write the proper equation

$$FV = \$50 \cdot \left[\frac{(1 + .005)^{24} - 1}{.005} \right] \quad \textbf{or} \quad FV = \$50 \cdot FVAF_{(0.5\%,\ 24)}$$

(example continued on next page)

19

Step 3. *Enter the data into the appropriate registers*

HP-10B	EL-733A	BA II Plus
-50.00 [PMT]	-50.00 [PMT]	-50.00 [PMT]
24.00 [N]	24.00 [n]	24.00 [N]
0.50 [I/YR]	0.50 [i]	0.5 [I/Y]
[FV] 1,271.60	[COMP] [FV] 1'271.60	[CPT] [FV] 1,271.60

Skye will have $1,271.60 in his account when he turns 16.

Two aspects of the cash flow diagram for ordinary annuities deserve emphasis. First, note that the first cash flow occurs at t=1, i.e., at the *end* of the first period. Second, payments continue up to and including t=24, at which point the future value is determined. The last payment is *not* compounded and is treated as though it was deposited and withdrawn simultaneously.

In Example 2-5, the periods were defined as months, which required you to use a *monthly* interest rate. The HP-10B and the BA II Plus are able to solve this problem in a more direct fashion using multiperiod compounding, which will be discussed later in this chapter.

Annuities Due

Annuities due are presented here for the sake of completeness, rather than to emphasize their importance. Example 2-6 is instructive because it illustrates difference in timing between cash flows at the beginning and end of periods.

2-6) It is New Year's Day and Zoe has resolved to keep better control of her finances during the coming year. Tomorrow morning she plans to open a holiday savings account with an initial deposit of $150. She plans to make **ten** more monthly deposits and withdraw her money on December 2nd in time for the holiday shopping season. Assume she earns interest at the rate of 1 percent per month. How much will she be able to spend?

Step 1. Construct a cash flow diagram

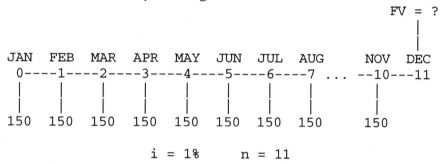

```
                                                        FV = ?
                                                         |
                                                         |
     JAN   FEB   MAR   APR   MAY   JUN   JUL   AUG      NOV   DEC
      0----1----2----3----4----5----6----7  ...  --10---11
      |     |     |     |     |     |     |     |        |
      |     |     |     |     |     |     |     |        |
     150   150   150   150   150   150   150   150      150

               i = 1%        n = 11
```

Step 2. Set BEGIN mode and enter the data into the appropriate registers

HP-10B	EL-733A	BA II Plus
		$\boxed{\text{2nd}}$ {BGN}
		$\boxed{\text{2nd}}$ {SET}
$\square$ {BEG/END}	$\boxed{\text{BGN}}$	$\boxed{\text{2nd}}$ {QUIT}
-150.00 $\boxed{\text{PMT}}$	-150.00 $\boxed{\text{PMT}}$	-150.00 $\boxed{\text{PMT}}$
11.00 $\boxed{\text{N}}$	11.00 $\boxed{\text{n}}$	11.00 $\boxed{\text{N}}$
1.00 $\boxed{\text{I/YR}}$	1.00 $\boxed{\text{i}}$	1.00 $\boxed{\text{I/Y}}$
$\boxed{\text{FV}}$ 1,752.38	$\boxed{\text{COMP}}$ $\boxed{\text{FV}}$ 1'752.38	$\boxed{\text{CPT}}$ $\boxed{\text{FV}}$ 1,752.38

Zoe will be able to spend $1,752.38 on holiday presents.

Note how the payment stream begins at t=0 and concludes one period before the future value is computed. The *number* of payments (n) is still eleven, even though the last payment occurs at t=10. In contrast to ordinary annuities, the last payment of an annuity due *is* compounded.

21

Present Value of an Ordinary Annuity

Present value of annuity problems are familiar to anyone who has ever taken out a closed-end loan, i.e., a loan which is repaid in a fixed number of payments. Example 2-7 shows how to determine the size of periodic payments.

2-7) Newlyweds Clayton and Deirdre are interested in financing a new car. At present, only Clayton has been able to find a job and the couple is experiencing some monetary constraints. Consequently, they are very concerned about the size of their monthly payment. The automobile dealer has proposed two alternatives to finance a $12,000 purchase: 1) 36 months at 6 percent interest or 2) 48 months at 12 percent interest. For the sake of simplicity, assume monthly compounding, i.e., simply divide the annual rates by 12 to get monthly rates. Which alternative offers the lower monthly payment?

Step 1.   Construct a cash flow diagram

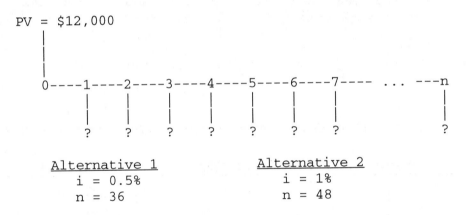

```
PV = $12,000
 |
 |
 |
 0----1----2----3----4----5----6----7----  ...  ---n
      |    |    |    |    |    |    |            |
      |    |    |    |    |    |    |            |
      ?    ?    ?    ?    ?    ?    ?            ?
```

Alternative 1	Alternative 2
i = 0.5%	i = 1%
n = 36	n = 48

Step 2.   Write the proper equations

<u>Alternative 1</u>:

$$\$12{,}000 = PMT \cdot \left[\frac{1 - \dfrac{1}{(1 + 0.005)^{36}}}{0.005} \right] \quad \textbf{or} \quad \$12{,}000 = PMT \cdot PVAF_{(0.5\%,\ 36)}$$

(example continued on next page)

Alternative 2:

$$\$12{,}000 = PMT \cdot \left[\frac{1 - \dfrac{1}{(1+0.01)^{48}}}{0.01}\right] \quad \textbf{or} \quad \$12{,}000 = PMT \cdot PVAF_{(1\%,\ 48)}$$

Step 3.   Enter the data into the appropriate registers

Alternative 1:

HP-10B	EL-733A	BA II Plus
12,000.00 [PV]	12'000.00 [PV]	12,000.00 [PV]
36.00 [N]	36.00 [n]	36.00 [N]
0.50 [I/YR]	0.50 [i]	0.50 [I/Y]
[PMT] −365.06	[COMP] [PMT] −365.06	[CPT] [PMT] −365.06

Alternative 2:

HP-10B	EL-733A	BA II Plus
12,000.00 [PV]	12'000.00 [PV]	12,000.00 [PV]
48.00 [N]	48.00 [n]	48.00 [N]
1.00 [I/YR]	1.00 [i]	1.00 [I/Y]
[PMT] −316.01	[COMP] [PMT] −316.01	[CPT] [PMT] −316.01

Alternative 1 has monthly payments of $365.06 while Alternative 2 has monthly payments of $316.01. Ignoring interest rate considerations and focusing only on payment size, Clayton and Deirdre should choose Alternative 2.

Solving for an Unknown Interest Rate

The superiority of financial calculators over Present Value/Future Value tables is most easily demonstrated when solving for unknown interest rates and unknown periods. Plugging values for FV, PV, and PMT into Equations 1' through 4' and solving frequently produces a factor NOT found in the tables. You're then forced to interpolate in order to obtain a (more-or-less) exact answer. Financial calculators use iteration to achieve a much closer approximation.

2-8) Ben's Pawn Shop makes 12-month personal loans in amounts up to $2,000. Ben requires equal monthly payments equal to one-tenth of the original loan amount. What monthly interest rate is Ben charging?

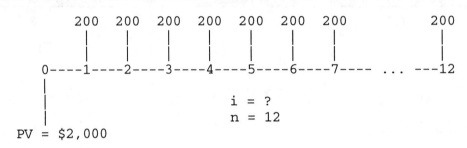

HP-10B		EL-733A		BA II Plus	
-2,000.00	PV	-2'000.00	PV	-2,000.00	PV
12.00	N	12.00	n	12.00	N
200.00	PMT	200.00	PMT	200.00	PMT
I/YR	2.92	COMP i	2.92	CPT I/Y	2.92

Ben charges a rather high monthly interest rate of 2.92 percent.

The answer to Example 2-8 is independent of the amount borrowed. To see this, try it again using a loan amount of $1,000 and $100 payments. Also, it is perfectly normal for display screens on the EL-733A and BA II Plus to go blank for 10-20 seconds while these calculators are "thinking."[6] The length of time serves as an indication of the difficulty involved in solving these problems manually.

---

[6]The display of the HP-10B flashes 'running' to announce it is calculating the answer.

Solving for an Unknown Number of Periods

Sometimes it is important to know how long it will take for a given sum to reach some future amount, or how many payments are remaining on an outstanding loan. Example 2-9 belongs to this class of problems.

2-9) Overpopulation is believed to be a significant factor leading to the degradation of Earth's environmental resources. The world population in 1992 was approximately 5.47 billion and was increasing at a rate of 1.7 percent per year. Some experts have estimated that the Earth can support no more than 8 billion people assuming current technology and patterns of resource utilization. If population growth rates are not slowed, when will this figure be achieved?

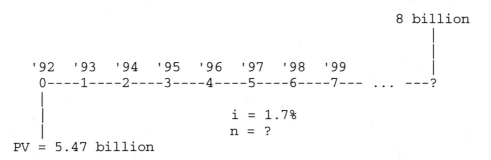

```
                                            8 billion
                                                |
                                                |
    '92  '93  '94  '95  '96  '97  '98  '99      |
    0----1----2----3----4----5----6----7--- ... ---?
    |
    |                        i = 1.7%
    |                        n = ?
    |
PV = 5.47 billion
```

HP-10B	EL-733A	BA II Plus
-5.47 [PV]	-5.47 [PV]	-5.47 [PV]
1.70 [I/YR]	1.70 [i]	1.70 [I/Y]
8.00 [FV]	8.00 [FV]	8.00 [FV]
[N] 22.55	[COMP] [n] 22.55	[CPT] [N] 22.55

If population growth remains unchecked, the Earth's human population will reach 8 million approximately 23 years from 1992, i.e., in the year 2015.

Example 2-9, besides providing food for thought, illustrates the usefulness of exponential functions in other disciplines. Populations grow in exactly the same fashion as interest.[7] The early economist Thomas Malthus (1766-1834) made just this point. He predicted that humanity was doomed to extinction since population increased at an exponential rate while food supplies and arable land increased at an arithmetic rate. (Malthus was wrong, partly because he failed to account for improvements in technology.)

---

[7]Populations will continue to grow exponentially only if resources are unlimited. In stable habitats with finite resources, populations frequently exhibit logistic, or S-shaped, growth.

Multiperiod Compounding

Before leaving the time value of money, a few words on interest rates are in order. In finance, payments are computed using either *simple interest* or *compound interest*. Under simple interest, a fixed percentage of the *original* principal is added to your account at the end of each period. Because simple interest is relatively easy to determine and because few institutions price their financial products in simple interest terms, it is mostly ignored in finance textbooks. All the examples up to now have dealt with *compound interest*, i.e., the situation in which interest accrues on the sum of principal and previously paid interest. Thus far, however, we have assumed that interest is compounded only once per period. This is not the general case. Interest can be compounded multiple times per period – many savings accounts, for instance, quote deposit rates in annual terms, "compounded daily."

Nominal and Effective Rates

Because compounding frequency changes the rate at which a sum of money grows or is discounted, it is important to distinguish between *nominal* and *effective* rates. *Nominal rate* is derived from the Latin word *nominum*, meaning name. Nominal rates are "in name only," and refer to the stated or posted rate found in advertising or contracts. An example of a nominal rate is: "12 percent, compounded quarterly." *Effective rates* are important because they allow you to determine the effects of multiperiod compounding. It seems logical that money deposited into an account paying "12 percent, compounded quarterly" would not grow to as large a figure as money in an account paying "12 percent, compounded monthly," and indeed this is so. Both accounts carry the same nominal rate – 12 percent – but the latter has the higher effective rate. Effective rates assume compounding occurs *once* per period. By converting nominal rates into effective rates, it is easy to compare the effects of different rates and compounding regimes. Equation 6 shows the relationship between nominal and effective rates:

$$k_{eff} = \left(1 + \frac{k_{nom}}{m}\right)^m - 1 \qquad (6)$$

where:
$$k_{eff} = \text{effective interest rate}$$
$$k_{nom} = \text{nominal interest rate}$$
$$m = \text{number of compounding sessions per period}$$

Built-in functions on the HP-10B, EL-733A and BA II Plus quickly convert between nominal and effective rates.[8]

---

[8]Don't forget to change back to single-period compounding (1 payment per period) afterwards!

2-10) Your local credit union advertises a 6 percent annual rate, compounded quarterly. What is the effective rate on these accounts?

$$k_{eff} = \left(1 + \frac{0.06}{4}\right)^4 - 1$$

HP-10B	EL-733A	BA II Plus
4.0000 ☐ {P/YR}	4.0000 [2ndF] {→EFF}	[2nd] {IConv}
6.0000 ☐ {NOM%}	6.0000	6.0000 [ENTER]
☐ {EFF%} 6.1364	[COMP] [=] 6.1364	[↓][↓]
		4.0000 [ENTER]
		[↑] [CPT] 6.1364

The effective rate equals 6.1364 percent.

Annual Percentage Rate (APR)

The United States' Truth in Lending Act (Regulation Z) was passed in 1968 to protect consumers from unscrupulous lenders. It established the *annual percentage rate* (APR) as a base rate for making comparisons between different financial instruments. Unfortunately, some misunderstandings exist concerning the APR and a closely related concept, the *effective annual rate* (EAR). The effective annual rate is the rate of interest that is earned on an investment if compounding occurs once per year. The APR is a *legal* attempt to operationalize the effective annual rate. In most cases, APR equals EAR.

The APR is instrument-dependent. Consider the case of a 5-year personal loan at 18 percent, compounded monthly and a credit card with interest charges of 1.5% per month. Both instruments have the same *effective annual rate:*

$$\textit{Loan: } \left(1 + \frac{0.18}{12}\right)^{12} - 1 = .1956 \Rightarrow 19.56 \text{ percent}$$

$$\textit{Credit Card: } (1 + .015)^{12} - 1 = .1956 \Rightarrow 19.56 \text{ percent}$$

but they have different APRs ...

$$Loan: \left(1 + \frac{0.18}{12}\right)^{12} - 1 = .1956 \Rightarrow 19.56 \text{ percent}$$

Credit Card: 1.5 x 12 = 18.00 percent

The loan is a form of closed-end credit, while charge cards are classified as revolving credit. The APR is *defined* differently for these two instruments. When making economic comparisons between interest rates, it is best to use the effective annual rate.[9]

Continuous Compounding

For a long time, US banks were prohibited from paying nominal deposit rates above a certain ceiling (Regulation Q). Bankers, in an effort to entice customers by offering higher effective rates, increased the frequency with which interest was compounded. Rates were compounded quarterly, then monthly, then weekly, then daily – where would it stop? The theoretical limit to the frequency with which interest rates can be compounded can be determined using calculus. At that limit, interest is said to be "compounded continuously."

Financial calculators do not directly convert between nominal rates and continuously compounded rates. Equations 7 and 8 and Example 2-11 are presented for the sake of completeness, rather than to illustrate use of the calculator's arithmetic functions. The relationship between present and future value is:

$$FV_t = PV \cdot e^{\gamma t} \qquad (7)$$

where:
γ = *continuously-compounded* nominal rate of return
e = base of natural logarithms
t = number of periods

Continuously compounded rates of return may be converted to effective annual rates (sometimes called *discrete* rates) for comparative purposes. Note that the continuously compounded nominal rate is *lower* than its equivalent effective annual rate of return. The relationship between continuously compounded and discrete rates is:

$$\gamma = \ln(1 + r) \quad \textbf{or} \quad r = e^{\gamma} - 1 \qquad (8)$$

where r is the effective annual (discrete) rate of return.

---

[9]The effective annual rate is but one of many *effective rates*. It is so called because it assumes compounding occurs once per *year*.

2-11) Catelyn deposited $2,000 into an IRA account at a local Savings and Loan exactly six years ago. Her account promised to pay interest at a rate of 8 percent, compounded *continuously*. How much should she have in her account *now*? What was Catelyn's equivalent effective annual rate?

$$FV = \$2,000 \ e^{(.08)(6)} = \$3,232.15$$

$$\text{effective annual rate} = r = e^{.08} - 1 = .0833 \ ==> 8.33 \text{ percent}$$

Multiperiod Compounding with the HP-10B and BA II Plus

Hewlett-Packard's HP-10B and Texas Instruments' BA II Plus allow users to solve problems involving multiperiod compounding in a more direct fashion. Recall Example 2-5, in which Skye plans to deposit $50 per month for 24 months into an account paying 6 percent annual interest in hopes of accruing enough money to buy a car. Interest is compounded monthly. The following keystrokes will solve this problem on the HP-10B and BA II Plus:

HP-10B		BA II Plus	
		2nd {P/Y}	
12.00 ☐ {P/YR}		12.00 ENTER 2nd {QUIT}	
−50.00 PMT		−50.00 PMT	
6.00 I/YR		6.00 I/Y	
24.00 N		24.00 N	
FV 1,271.60		CPT FV 1,271.60	

The sole effect of the {P/YR} or {P/Y} keys is to divide values in the interest rate register by the number of payment periods per year. This procedure is NOT recommended because: 1) It can create additional errors if you forget to change the compounding frequency back and 2) It "mixes apples with pears" – note that the payment and time to maturity are expressed in terms of *periods* (months, in this case) while the yield is expressed per *year*.

Perpetuities

The field of finance has a few examples where cash flows are assumed to continue *ad infinitum*. None of the three calculators covered in this book is hardwired to solve for an infinite series of cash flows. The author would be remiss, however, if he failed to include the requisite formula and an example illustrating its use:

$$\text{PV of a perpetuity} = \frac{\text{PMT}}{i} \tag{9}$$

2-12) Former US President John F. Kennedy's grave in Arlington Cemetery is marked by an "eternal flame," which has burned continuously since his assassination in 1963. Suppose that annual fuel expenses were estimated at $1,200 per year, and the annual interest rate at that time was 5 percent. How much should this portion of the monument have cost at the time of its construction?

$$\text{PV} = \frac{\$1,200}{.05} = \$24,000$$

Assuming constant interest rates and constant annual expenses for fuel, the US government should have spent $24,000 on this portion of the monument.

The Principle of Additivity

The Principle of Additivity allows you to express just about any pattern of cash flows using the four basic equations as "building blocks." Cash flows may be compounded forward or discounted backward to obtain equivalent values at a common point in time, which can then be added or subtracted from one another. Annuity streams can be similarly "collapsed" into single-period cash flows, which can be further manipulated into values at yet a different point in time. This two-step process is sometimes called "double-compounding" or "double-discounting."

2-13) Antonio concluded his military training with the Swiss army exactly two years ago. During his 18-month period of service, he was able to deposit SFr 75,- at the end of each month into an account paying 6 percent interest, compounded monthly. How much money is in his account **now**?

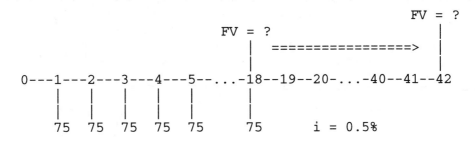

$$75 \cdot \text{FVAF}_{(0.5\%,18)} \cdot \text{FVIF}_{(0.5\%,24)} = \text{Future Value at } t=42$$

This problem must be solved in two steps. First, the FV of an annuity at t=18 must be determined. Then, that value must be compounded forward two years (24 periods) to arrive at Antonio's current balance.

HP-10B		EL-733A		BA II Plus	
-75.00	PMT	-75.00	PMT	-75.00	PMT
18.00	N	18.00	n	18.00	N
0.50	I/YR	0.50	i	0.5	I/Y
FV	1,408.93	COMP FV	1'408.93	CPT FV	1,408.93

HP-10B		EL-733A		BA II Plus	
-1,408.93	PV	-1'408.93	PV	-1,408.93	PV
24.00	N	24.00	n	24.00	N
0.50	I/YR	0.50	i	0.5	I/Y
FV	1,588.09	COMP FV	1'588.09	CPT FV	1,588.09

Antonio should have approximately 1,588 Swiss francs in his account.

Example 2-13 is interesting because it illustrates differences between effective and nominal rates and "double compounding" simultaneously. In some cases, it is easier to look up the appropriate interest rate factors and multiply them all together than to use an electronic calculator (unfortunately, few Present Value/Future Value tables contain factors for 0.5 percent).

The Principle of Additivity is also used to solve Example 2-14, the famous "birthday problem."

2-14) Today is Rob's birthday and he decides to start saving for his college education. Rob plans to begin college on his 18th birthday and will need $6,000 per year at the **beginning** of each of the next four years. He will make a deposit one year from today into an account paying 12 percent annual interest, and continue to make an identical deposit each year *up to and including the year he begins college*. If annual deposits of $3,212.89 will allow Rob to reach his goal, what birthday is he celebrating today?

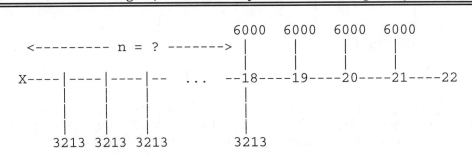

Obviously, this is a contrived problem. However, it is useful for illustrating the application of both equations and calculator solutions. A first step is to determine a common point to evaluate both streams of cash flows.

$$3{,}212.89 \cdot \text{FVAF}_{(12\%,n)} = \text{value of accumulated savings at t=18}$$

$$6{,}000 \cdot \text{PVAF}_{(12\%,3)} + 6{,}000 = \text{value of prospective expenses at t=18}$$

The second equation may be solved as written or as an annuity due using the following keystrokes:

HP-10B	EL-733A	BA II Plus
		2nd {BGN}
		2nd {SET}
☐ {BEG/END}	BGN	2nd {QUIT}
-6,000.00 PMT	-6'000.00 PMT	-6,000.00 PMT
4.00 N	4.00 n	4.00 N
12.00 I/YR	12.00 i	12.00 I/Y
PV 20,410.99	COMP PV 20'410.99	CPT PV 20,410.99

(example continued on next page)

Setting the present value of expenditures equal to the future value of the savings and solving for n gives the number of years between today and Rob's 18th birthday. (Don't forget to set your calculator back to "END" mode before entering these keystrokes).

HP-10B	EL-733A	BA II Plus
-3,212.89 PMT	-3'212.89 PMT	-3,212.89 PMT
20,410.99 FV	20'410.99 FV	20,410.99 FV
12.00 I/YR	12.00 i	12.00 I/Y
N 5.00	COMP n 5.00	CPT N 5.00

Since n = 5, today must be Rob's 13th birthday.

Chapter Three

VALUATION OF FINANCIAL INSTRUMENTS

"A million dollars is not what it used to be."

– Howard Hughes, 1937

Financial instruments are nothing more than standardized sets of specific cash flow patterns. The previous chapter showed how a financial calculator could be used to solve general problems involving the time value of money. This chapter provides additional insight into the pricing of bonds, common stocks, preferred stocks and mortgage instruments.

The Discounted Cash Flow Model

Theoretically, a security's price equals the present value of its expected future cash inflows. The discounted cash flow (DCF) model expresses the price of a security as the sum of its future discounted cash flows:

$$\text{Price} = \sum_{t=1}^{n} \frac{CF_t}{(1+i)^t} \tag{1}$$

where: CF_t = cash flow at time t
   i = interest rate per period
   t = period in which a given cash flow is received[1]

The discount rate is also known as the *capitalization rate* or *required rate of return*; it reflects the *minimum* return required by investors. In practice, prices are set by the interaction of supply and demand and reflect investors' best *estimates* of future cash flows and interest rates.

Pure Discount Securities

Pure discount securities promise a single cash flow at some time in the future. Examples include Certificates of Deposit (CDs), zero coupon bonds (zeros), Treasury bills and simple IOUs. Prices of pure discount securities are easily determined using a financial calculator's time value of money registers.

----

[1]Note that t need NOT be an integer.

3-1) A local furniture store advertises that it will give a $1,000 bond to anyone purchasing a complete dining room set during a certain period of time. Upon reading the fine print, you discover that the bond in question is a zero-coupon bond which promises to make a single $1,000 payment ten years in the future. Assuming an annual discount rate of 8 percent, what is this bond worth **now**?

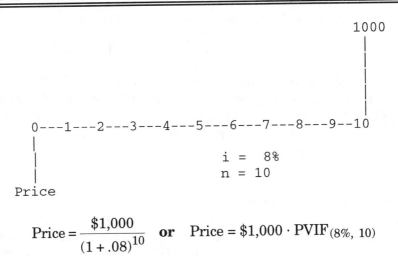

$$\text{Price} = \frac{\$1,000}{(1+.08)^{10}} \quad \textbf{or} \quad \text{Price} = \$1,000 \cdot \text{PVIF}_{(8\%,\ 10)}$$

HP-10B	EL-733A	BA II Plus
1,000.00 $\boxed{\text{FV}}$	1′000.00 $\boxed{\text{FV}}$	1,000.00 $\boxed{\text{FV}}$
10.00 $\boxed{\text{N}}$	10.00 $\boxed{\text{n}}$	10.00 $\boxed{\text{N}}$
8.00 $\boxed{\text{I/YR}}$	8.00 $\boxed{\text{i}}$	8.00 $\boxed{\text{I/Y}}$
$\boxed{\text{PV}}$ -463.19	$\boxed{\text{COMP}}$ $\boxed{\text{PV}}$ -463.19	$\boxed{\text{CPT}}$ $\boxed{\text{PV}}$ -463.19

Assuming one could find a buyer, the bond should be valued at $463.19.

Simple Bond Pricing

So-called "simple" bond pricing problems occur when bonds are purchased on exact coupon payment dates. As most bonds pay interest but once or twice per year, such occasions are obviously rare in practice (but incredibly common in finance textbooks). The "bond equation," mentioned briefly in Chapter Two, is a common way of expressing a bond's price as the present value of its future cash flows. It has a further advantage, in that problems of this sort can be solved using only the time value of money registers. Essentially, bonds can be viewed as a level annuity with a 'tail,' or additional inflow occurring at maturity. Figure 3-1 presents a simple example of a cash flow pattern appropriate for a newly issued annual coupon bond.

Figure 3-1. An Annual Coupon Bond

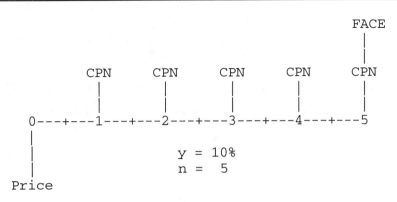

Several aspects of Figure 3-1 are worthy of note. First, the term "Price" has replaced "Present Value." Finance theory holds that the best estimate of an asset's price is the discounted value of its expected future cash flows. Second, 'y' has replaced 'i' as the variable corresponding to the interest rate used to discount future cash flows. This reflects the securities industry's practice of referring to bond *yields* as opposed to interest or discount rates. Third, future cash flows come in the form of coupon payments (CPN) and return of principal (FACE, or PAR). The cash flow at t=5 is composed of both CPN and FACE payments. A few other definitions may help prevent confusion:

> *par value:* stated face value of a bond, usually $1,000, representing the amount of money a firm borrows and promises to repay at a later date … also known as "face value" or "maturity value"
>
> *maturity date:* date when principal must be repaid
>
> *coupon rate:* interest payment, expressed as a *percentage* of par value
>
> *coupon payment:* dollar amount of interest payment
>
> *yield to maturity:* discount rate equating the price of a bond with the present value of the interest and principal payments (equivalent to the *internal rate of return*) … also known as "interest on interest"

A bond's yield to maturity is the return promised to an investor *so long as the issuer meets all interest and principal payments on time* **and** the investor *reinvests the coupon income at an average rate of return equal to the computed yield.* Note that the yield to maturity is **not** the same as a bond's coupon rate or interest rate. Yields are important because bond prices are frequently expressed in terms of yield, rather than as a dollar price. The higher *(lower)* a bond's price, the *lower (higher)* its yield to maturity.

As an illustration of simple bond pricing, consider Example 3-2. The present value of the future cash flows can be determined as the sum of the present values of **either** 1) A 4-period annuity of $100 plus $1,100 at t=5 **or** 2) A 5-period annuity of $100 plus $1,000 at t=5. Alternative 2 is preferable when using a financial calculator, as bond prices or yields can be calculated in a single step.

3-2) How much should you pay for a 10 percent, annual coupon bond maturing in exactly 5 years? It is currently yielding 8 percent.

Step 1. Draw the cash flow diagram

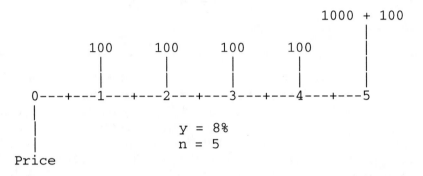

Step 2. Write the appropriate equation

$$\text{Price} = \$100 \cdot \left[\frac{1 - \dfrac{1}{(1+.08)^5}}{.08} \right] + \frac{\$1,000}{(1+.08)^5} \quad \textbf{or}$$

$$\text{Price} = \$100 \cdot \text{PVAF}_{(8\%,\ 5)} + \$1,000 \cdot \text{PVIF}_{(8\%,\ 5)}$$

Step 3. Enter the data into the appropriate registers

HP-10B	EL-733A	BA II Plus
100.00 `PMT`	100.00 `PMT`	100.00 `PMT`
1,000.00 `FV`	1'000.00 `FV`	1,000.00 `FV`
5.00 `N`	5.00 `n`	5.00 `N`
8.00 `I/YR`	8.00 `i`	8.00 `I/Y`
`PV` -1,079.85	`COMP` `PV` -1'079.85	`CPT` `PV` -1,079.85

You should pay $1,079.85 for a bond with these characteristics.

Example 3-2 highlights an interesting characteristic of bonds that can be used to spot-check your answers. A bond will sell at a *premium* (i.e., a price above its par value) whenever its coupon rate is greater than investors' required yield. Bonds sell at a discount (i.e., below par value) when required rates of return exceed coupon rates. When a bond's yield to maturity exactly equals its coupon rate, it is priced at face value. In Example 3-2, the bond's coupon rate (10 percent) exceeds investors' required yield (8 percent), which caused it to sell for more than its assumed par value of $1,000.[2]

Bond Yields

The usefulness of financial calculators becomes readily apparent when solving for bond yields. Solving the "bond equations" for yield to maturity is a trial and error process in which you first choose an interest rate, then compute the present value of the expected future cash inflows and compare this number with the bond's price. If they are not exactly equal, a different interest rate is selected and the process is repeated. Eventually, through iteration, differences between the calculated present value and a known price become so small that they're effectively equal. Unfortunately, it can take a lot of time to perform these repetitive calculations.

Financial calculators follow exactly the same logic to arrive at a yield to maturity, but because they are hardwired to perform these specific types of calculations, they are able to arrive at a precise answer much more swiftly.

---

[2]Unless specifically told otherwise, one should generally assume a par value of $1,000 for all US corporate, municipal and government bonds.

3-3) What is the yield to maturity on a 7 percent, annual coupon bond maturing in exactly 4 years? It is currently selling for $850.

Step 1. Draw the cash flow diagram

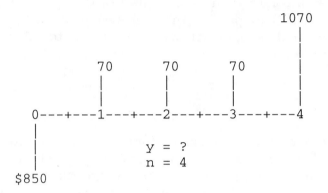

Step 2. Write the appropriate equation

$$\$850 = \$70 \cdot \left[\frac{1 - \dfrac{1}{(1+y)^4}}{y}\right] + \frac{\$1,000}{(1+y)^5} \quad \textbf{or}$$

$$\text{Price} = \$70 \cdot \text{PVAF}_{(y\%,\ 4)} + \$1,000 \cdot \text{PVIF}_{(y\%,\ 4)}$$

Step 3. Enter the data into the appropriate registers

HP-10B		EL-733A		BA II Plus	
−850.00	PV	−850.00	PV	−850.00	PV
70.00	PMT	70.00	PMT	70.00	PMT
1,000.00	FV	1'000.00	FV	1,000.00	FV
4.00	N	4.00	n	4.00	N
I/YR 11.93		COMP i 11.93		CPT I/Y 11.93	

This bond is priced to yield 11.93 percent. The value agrees with its status as a discount bond, i.e., coupon rate < bond yield.

Semiannual Compounding

Most bonds issued in the United States pay interest semiannually, or twice per year. Only *Eurobonds* (domestic currency bonds issued inside a foreign country) are well known for making annual interest payments. Coupon rates, however, are nearly always expressed on an annual basis, as are bond yields. Thus, it's generally a good idea to convert years into semiannual payment periods before beginning a problem.

3-4) How much should you pay to purchase a 5 percent, semiannual coupon bond maturing in exactly four years? Similar bonds are priced to yield 4 percent.

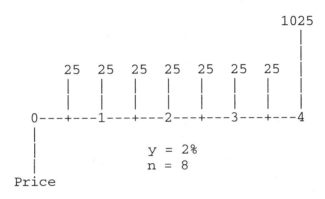

$$\text{Price} = \$25 \cdot \left[\frac{1 - \dfrac{1}{(1 + .02)^8}}{.02}\right] + \frac{\$1,000}{(1 + .02)^8} \quad \textbf{or}$$

$$\text{Price} = \$25 \cdot \text{PVAF}_{(2\%,\ 8)} + \$1,000 \cdot \text{PVIF}_{(2\%,\ 8)}$$

HP-10B		EL-733A		BA II Plus	
25.00	PMT	25.00	PMT	25.00	PMT
1,000.00	FV	1'000.00	FV	1,000.00	FV
8.00	N	8.00	n	8.00	N
2.00	I/YR	2.00	i	2.00	I/Y
PV −1,036.63		COMP PV −1'036.63		CPT PV −1,036.63	

The bond is worth $1,036.63.

The same logic is applied when solving for bond yields:

3-5) A 5-year, 6 percent semiannual coupon bond is currently selling for $900. What is its yield to maturity?

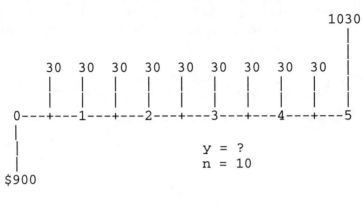

$$\$900 = \$30 \cdot \left[\frac{1 - \dfrac{1}{(1+y)^{10}}}{y} \right] + \frac{\$1,000}{(1+y)^{10}} \quad \textbf{or}$$

$$\$900 = \$30 \cdot \text{PVAF}_{(y\%,\ 10)} + \$1,000 \cdot \text{PVIF}_{(y\%,\ 10)}$$

HP-10B	EL-733A	BA II Plus
-900.00 [PV]	-900.00 [PV]	-900.00 [PV]
30.00 [PMT]	30.00 [PMT]	30.00 [PMT]
1,000.00 [FV]	1'000.00 [FV]	1,000.00 [FV]
10.00 [N]	10.00 [n]	10.00 [N]
[I/YR] 4.25	[COMP] [i] 4.25	[CPT] [I/Y] 4.25

Remember that the answer is expressed *per period*. The *effective* annual yield to maturity = $(1.0425)^2$ - 1, or 8.68 percent. In practice, the periodic yield is generally doubled as an approximation ... 2 x 4.25 = 8.50 percent.

The ability of the HP-10B and BA II Plus to handle multiple payments per period can be used in solving simple bond problems, though you must be careful in interpreting the results. For instance, the following keystroke sequences correspond to Example 3-5; note that the answer is expressed as a *nominal* yield to maturity.

HP-10B		**BA II Plus**	
			2nd {P/Y}
2.00	☐ {P/YR}	2.00 ENTER	2nd {QUIT}
-900.00	PV	-900.00	PV
30.00	PMT	30.00	PMT
1,000.00	FV	1,000.00	FV
10.00	N	10.00	N
I/YR	8.50	CPT I/Y	8.50

"Advanced" bond pricing functions are required to price bonds purchased at times other than coupon anniversary dates. Of the calculators covered in this book, only the BA II Plus has the built-in date functions necessary for this task.[3]

Preferred Stock

Most preferred stock pays regular, fixed dividends for an indefinite period of time. Because dividends are assumed to be paid forever, its price may be found using the formula for a perpetuity. Dividends may be quoted either as a *dollar amount* or as a *percentage of par*.

$$\text{Price of preferred stock} = \frac{\text{Preferred dividend (in dollars)}}{\text{Required return (as a decimal)}}$$

No special techniques (other than an understanding of basic algebra) are needed to solve these problems on an electronic calculator. *Perpetual bonds* also pay interest in this manner and are priced in the same way.

---

[3]See Chapter 5 in the *BA II Plus Guidebook*. These functions are also found on more advanced Hewlett-Packard calculators.

Common Stock

Unlike preferred stock, dividends on common stock are not required to be paid and generally are not constant over subsequent periods of time. Valuation of common stock is perhaps more art than science and must take into account investor preferences and performance vís-a-vís other equity securities.

A common method for valuing common stock is to assume an infinite series of dividends growing at some constant rate. This particular pattern of cash flows, a constantly growing perpetuity, can be expressed as a simple closed-form equation:

$$\text{Price of common stock at time } 0 = \frac{\text{Dividend in period 1}}{(\text{Required return} - \text{growth rate})}$$

The *dividend growth model* also assumes investors' required rate of return exceeds the dividend growth rate. As was the case with preferred stock, financial calculators are able to assist in performing algebraic calculations but are not specifically programmed to solve this model.

Mortgage Instruments

Mortgage debt represents the largest and fastest-growing component of the capital markets. Technically, a mortgage is a *pledge* of [real] property used to secure payment of a debt. It is quite common, however, to hear the term mortgage used in reference to the debt instrument, or mortgage loan, itself. In keeping with actual practice, the latter interpretation is used in this book.

There are many, many different kinds of mortgages with all sorts of interesting characteristics. Pass-through certificates, mortgage-backed bonds and collateralized mortgage obligations further complicate mortgage taxonomies. Sample calculations for three common aspects of mortgage loans – amortization, balloon payments and prepaid points – are presented in the following sections.

Loan Amortization

The term "amortization" is derived from the Latin *mort*, meaning death. In one sense, amortized loans are 'killed off' over time by making a series of payments. In an amortized loan, payments remain constant, although their composition changes. The part of a payment representing interest *declines* over the life of the loan, while the part representing principal *increases*. The payment pattern for an amortized loan is illustrated in Figure 3-2.

Figure 3-2. Loan Amortization

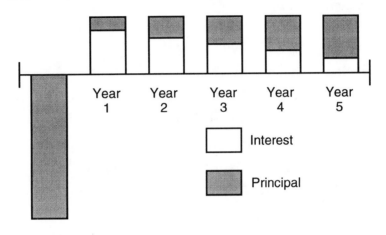

Because the repayment of interest and principal are treated differently under US tax law, it is often important to know exactly what portion of a given payment represents principal and what portion represents interest. An amortization schedule is used to determine this. There are three basic relationships that are used in preparing an amortization schedule:

$$\frac{\text{Interest}}{\text{Portion}} = \text{Interest Rate} \times \text{Previous Balance} \qquad (2a)$$

$$\frac{\text{Principal}}{\text{Portion}} = \text{Payment} - \text{Interest} \qquad (2b)$$

$$\frac{\text{Ending}}{\text{Balance}} = \frac{\text{Beginning}}{\text{Balance}} - \frac{\text{Accumulated Principal}}{\text{Payments}} \qquad (2c)$$

A complete amortization schedule is derived by repeated application of these equations (Example 3-6).

3-6) Prepare an amortization schedule for a $10,000 five-year loan at 15 percent annual interest.

Step 1: Determine the annual payment

$$\$10,000 = \text{PMT} \cdot \text{PVAF}_{(15\%,\ 5)}$$

$$\text{PMT} = \$2,983.16$$

Step 2: Amortize the loan

Interest$_1$ = .15 · $10,000 = $1,500

Principal$_1$ = $2,983.16 − 1,500 = $1,483.16

Ending Balance$_1$ = $10,000 − 1,483.16 = $8,516.84

Interest$_2$ = .15 · $8,516.84 = $1,277.53

Principal$_2$ = $2,983.15 − 1,277.53 = $1,705.63

Ending Balance$_2$ = $8,516.84 − 1,705.63 = $6,811.22

… and so on …

	Payment		**Ending**
	Interest	*Principal*	**Balance**
Year 1	$ 1,500.00	$ 1,483.16	$ 8,516.84
Year 2	1,277.53	1,705.63	6,811.22
Year 3	1,021.68	1,961.47	4,849.74
Year 4	727.46	2,255.69	2,594.05
Year 5	389.11	2,594.05	$0.00

Financial calculators are perfect tools for completing this repetitious task. Moreover, they are able to quickly determine the composition of *any* particular payment quickly and easily without engaging in such laborious calculations. The following tables illustrate how to use the HP-10B, EL-733A and BA II Plus in solving the previous problem.

Hewlett Packard HP-10B

-10,000.00 [PV]

15.00 [I/YR]

5.00 [N]

[PMT] 2,983.16

1 [INPUT] [☐] {AMORT} [=] 1,500.00 <== Interest

[=] 1,483.16 <== Principal

[=] -8,516.84 <== Balance @ t=1

2 [INPUT] [☐] {AMORT} [=] 1,277.53 <== Interest

[=] 1,705.63 <== Principal

[=] -6,811.21 <== Balance @ t=2

etc.

Sharp Electronics EL-733A

-10'000.00 [PV]

15.00 [i]

5.00 [n]

[COMP] [PMT] 2'983.15

1 [AMRT] 1'483.15 <== Principal

[AMRT] 1'500.00 <== Interest

[AMRT] -8'516.84 <== Balance @ t=1

2 [AMRT] 1'705.63 <== Principal

[AMRT] 1'277.53 <== Interest

[AMRT] -6'811.22 <== Balance @ t=2

etc.

-10,000.00 $\boxed{\text{PV}}$

15.00 $\boxed{\text{I/Y}}$

5.00 $\boxed{\text{N}}$

$\boxed{\text{CPT}}$ $\boxed{\text{PMT}}$ 2,983.16

$\boxed{\text{2nd}}$ {Amort} $\boxed{\text{2nd}}$ {CLR Work}

1 $\boxed{\text{ENTER}}$ $\boxed{\downarrow}$

1 $\boxed{\text{ENTER}}$ $\boxed{\downarrow}$ -8,516.84 <== Balance @ t=1

$\boxed{\downarrow}$ 1,483.16 <== Principal

$\boxed{\downarrow}$ 1,500.00 <== Interest

$\boxed{\downarrow}$

2 $\boxed{\text{ENTER}}$ $\boxed{\downarrow}$

2 $\boxed{\text{ENTER}}$ $\boxed{\downarrow}$ -6,811.21 <== Balance @ t=2

$\boxed{\downarrow}$ -1,705.63 <== Principal

$\boxed{\downarrow}$ -1,277.53 <== Interest

etc.

Each of these calculators reports the interest, principal and remaining balance in a slightly different fashion. Example 3-7 shows how financial calculators can be used to solve a particularly tedious problem.

3-7) Thomas and Edeltraud have just signed a DM 375,000 mortgage loan at a 12 percent nominal rate of interest. They will be required to make monthly payments for the next 30 years. What portion of the 8th payment represents principal? How much interest will the couple have paid at the end of the first *year*, i.e., at the end of 12 months?

$$\text{DM } 375,000 = \text{PMT} \cdot \text{PVAF}_{(1\%, \, 360)}$$

$$\text{PMT} = \text{DM } 3,857.30$$

(example continued on next page)

Hewlett Packard HP-10B

$$-375{,}000.00 \quad \boxed{\text{PV}}$$

$$1.00 \quad \boxed{\text{I/YR}}$$

$$360.00 \quad \boxed{\text{N}}$$

$$\boxed{\text{PMT}} \quad 3{,}857.30$$

Principal   portion   of   8th

payment	-3,742.26	<== Interest
8 $\boxed{\text{INPUT}}$ $\boxed{}$ {AMORT} $\boxed{=}$	- 115.04	<== Principal
$\boxed{=}$	-374,110.95	<== Balance @ t=8
$\boxed{=}$		

Interest   from   t=1   to   t=12   44,926.77   <== Total interest

1 $\boxed{\text{INPUT}}$ 12 $\boxed{}$ {AMORT} $\boxed{=}$	1,360.83	<== Principal
$\boxed{=}$	-373,639.17	<== Balance @ t=12
$\boxed{=}$		

(example continued on next page)

Sharp Electronics EL-733A

```
-375'000.00  PV
       1.00  i
     360.00  n
  COMP  PMT  3'857.30
```

Principal portion of 8th

```
        payment       115.04    <== Principal
      8  AMRT        3'742.26    <== Interest
         AMRT     -374'110.97    <== Balance @ t=8
         AMRT
```

Interest from t=1 to t=12

```
                      1'360.80   <== Principal
  1  P₁/P₂  12  P₁/P₂  ACC  44'926.77   <== Total interest
              ACC
```

(example continued on next page)

Texas Instruments BA II Plus

-375,000.00 [PV]

1.00 [I/Y]

360.00 [N]

[CPT] [PMT] 3,857.30

[2nd] {Amort} [2nd] {CLR Work}

Principal portion of 8th payment

8	[ENTER] [↓]	-374,110.95	<== Balance @ t=8
8	[ENTER] [↓]	115.04	<== Principal
	[↓]	3,742.26	<== Interest
	[↓]		

Interest from t=1 to t=12

[2nd] {CLR Work}

1	[ENTER] [↓]	-373,639.17	<== Balance @ t=12
12	[ENTER] [↓]	1,360.83	<== Principal
	[↓]	44,926.77	<== Total interest
	[↓]		

Balloon Payments

Balloon mortgages differ from ordinary mortgages in that the principal is not wholly amortized. Rather, a part of it is repaid in a lump sum (the "balloon") at some time in the future. The cash flows associated with balloon mortgages closely resemble the "bond pattern," and indeed, that is how these problems should be solved.

3-8) Kent and Kristin are considering the purchase of an apartment building that will be financed by a $650,000 loan at 8.0 percent, compounded monthly. A balloon payment of $500,000 is due at the end of five years. What is their monthly payment amount?

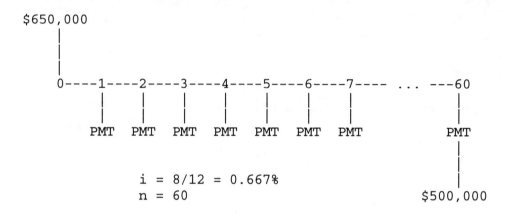

$$\$650,000 = \text{PMT} \cdot \text{PVAF}_{(8/12\%,\ 360)} + \$500,000 \cdot \text{PVIF}_{(8/12\%,\ 360)}$$

HP-10B		EL-733A		BA II Plus	
650,000	PV	650'000	PV	650,000	PV
−500,000	FV	−500'000	FV	−500,000	FV
60	N	60	n	60	N
0.667	I/YR	0.667	i	0.667	I/Y
PMT	−6,376.75	COMP PMT	−6'376.75	CPT PMT	−6,376.75

Kent and Kristin's payments are approximately $6,376.75 per month.

Sometimes lenders require a borrower to make an immediate cash payment at the loan's inception. These payments are frequently calculated as a percentage of the outstanding loan amount and expressed as "points," where each point equals one percent of the total loan value.[4] Points increase a lender's effective yield (and a borrower's effective cost!) because some of the outstanding principal is repaid immediately. A classic problem in mortgage lending is to calculate the effective yield of a loan with points.

3-9) Ron and Wendy have applied for a 20-year, $100,000 mortgage loan at a fixed rate of 10 percent. Their bank charges a front-end fee of 3 points. Compute the effective annual rate on this loan assuming monthly payments and no prepayment, i.e., the loan runs the full 20-year term.

$$\$100,000 = \text{PMT} \cdot \text{PVAF}_{(10/12\%, \, 240)}$$

$$\text{PMT} = \$965.02$$

$$\$100,000 - .03 \cdot \$100,000 = \$97,000$$

```
$97,000
  |
  |                    i = ?
  |                    n = 240
  |
  0----1----2----3----4----5----6----7----  ... --240
       |    |    |    |    |    |    |           |
       |    |    |    |    |    |    |           |
      965  965  965  965  965  965  965         965
```

HP-10B	EL-733A	BA II Plus
-97,000.00 [PV]	-97'000.00 [PV]	-97,000.00 [PV]
965.02 [PMT]	965.02 [PMT]	965.02 [PMT]
240.00 [N]	240.00 [n]	240.00 [N]
[I/YR] 0.871	[COMP] [i] 0.871	[CPT] [I/Y] 0.871

The effective annual rate equals $(1.00871)^{12} - 1 = 0.11$ or 11 percent.

---

[4]"Basis points" are slightly different. One percentage point equals 100 basis points.

Chapter Four

USING THE CASH FLOW REGISTERS

O'Donnell's Three Laws of Finance

1. Get the cash.

2. Get the cash.

3. Get the cash.

The well-known torch singer Sophie Tucker reputedly once said, "I've been rich and I've been poor, and let me tell you, rich is better." In either case, a calculator's cash flow registers would have been helpful for computing the value and/or yield of unusual cash flow patterns. 'Standard' cash flow patterns, e.g., those discussed in Chapter Two and illustrated in Appendix A, are generally best solved using the time value of money (TVM) registers. When a series of cash flows doesn't readily fit into one of the standard patterns, it may be time to use the cash flow registers. Cash flow registers are extremely useful in valuing the uneven payment streams often found in capital budgeting problems.

The cash flow registers are simultaneously more flexible and more constraining than the TVM registers. They are more flexible because you are not limited to simple patterns of annuities, present values and future values. On the other hand, they are only capable of determining two things: the value at t=0 of a future stream of cash flows and the interest rate equating a stream of future cash flows with a specified initial outlay. It is *not* possible to solve for unknown payment amounts or time periods as it is with the TVM registers.

Conceptually, the cash flow registers are quite different from the TVM registers. First, order is important. The first cash flow you enter is assumed to occur at t=0 and is called the *initial outlay,* because it generally represents an investment of funds. It is abbreviated as I_0 or CF_0. Second, the *frequency* of each cash flow (except the initial outlay) must be specified. This is a handy feature when a project is associated with a long series of identical cash flows.[1] Third, *signs* are extremely important. Cash outflows are entered as negative numbers, while cash inflows must be positive. If you are solving for Net Present Value, you must also specify an appropriate discount rate in the interest rate register. The major use of the cash flow registers is in evaluating investment projects using the Net Present Value (NPV) and Internal Rate of Return (IRR) decision criteria.

---

[1]Frequencies are handled somewhat differently across calculator models. They are optional on the HP-10B. On the BA II Plus, you must specify the frequency after *every* cash flow. The EL-733A requires frequencies be entered *before* the cash flow itself.

Net Present Value

Net present value (NPV) reflects the difference between the sum of the present values of the project's discounted future cash flows and its initial outlay. Mathematically, it is defined as:

$$NPV = \sum_{t=1}^{n} \frac{CF_t}{(1+i)^t} - I_0 \qquad (1)$$

where:
$\quad$ NPV $\;=\;$ net present value
$\quad$ CF_t $\;=\;$ cash flow at time t
$\quad$ I_0 $\;=\;$ initial outlay
$\quad\quad$ i $\;=\;$ discount rate or "required rate of return"
$\quad\quad\quad\quad$ or "cost of capital" or "hurdle rate"

The NPV decision rule is to *accept* projects with positive or zero NPVs and to *reject* projects with negative NPVs. For mutually exclusive projects, choose the one with the higher NPV, *unless* capital rationing is a consideration. The discount rate, i, depends upon the project's risk. Required returns increase with increasing project risk. It is assumed that future cash flows can be reinvested at the project's cost of capital.

Most students find it relatively easy to use the cash flow registers in solving net present value problems. The primary hurdle is in setting up the problem and specifying which cash flows go where. Example 4-1 illustrates the application of net present value analysis.

4-1) Matthew 16:26 asks, "What does it profit a man if he gain the world but lose his soul?" Assume the World, valued at $105, will be gained now, and the Soul, worth $121, will be lost at t=2. According to the NPV criterion, what decision should a man make, assuming a discount rate of 10 percent?

Step 1. Draw a cash flow diagram showing cash inflows and outflows

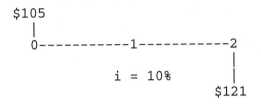

Step 2. Write an equation describing the series of cash flows

$$NPV = + \$105 + \frac{\$0}{(1.10)^1} - \frac{\$121}{(1.10)^2}$$

*Step 3. Enter the data into the cash flow registers – note that in this case, the initial outlay is **positive** and $CF_1 = 0$*

HP-10B	EL-733A	BA II Plus		
105.00 [CFj]	105.00 [CFi]	[CF]		
0.00 [CFj]	0.00 [CFi]	[2nd] {CLR Work}		
-121.00 [CFj]	-121.00 [CFi]	105.00 [ENTER] [↓]		
10.00 [I/YR]	10.00 [i]	0.00 [ENTER] [↓]		
[ ] {NPV} 5.00	[NPV] 5.00	1.00 [ENTER] [↓]		
		-121.00 [ENTER] [↓]		
		1.00 [ENTER] [↓]		
		[NPV]		
		10.00 [ENTER]		
		[↓] [CPT] 5.00		

Under these assumptions, it will profit a man $5.00 to gain the World.

Internal Rate of Return

A project's *internal rate of return* (IRR) is determined as the interest rate equating the sum of the discounted future cash flows with the initial outlay. Developed by Kenneth Boulding in 1935, the internal rate of return provides a useful way of assessing a project's profitability in terms of an "average" discounted return over a given period of time. When IRR equals the discount rate, net present value equals zero (Figure 4-1).

Figure 4-1. NPV and IRR

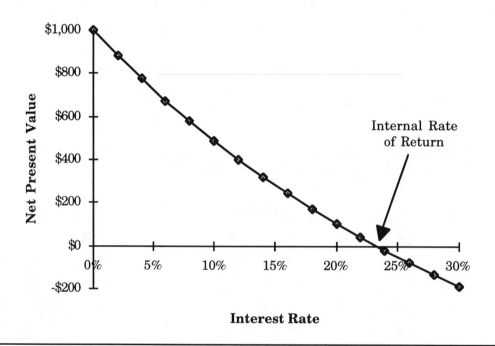

The internal rate of return criterion assumes a project's cash flows are reinvested at the IRR itself. In this sense, it is equivalent to a bond's "yield to maturity." Solving for the IRR without some sort of electronic aid is very tedious, and becomes more difficult as variability in a cash flow series increases. Essentially, you must search iteratively for an interest rate that equates both sides of Equation 2.

$$I_0 = \sum_{t=1}^{n} \frac{CF_t}{(1 + IRR)^t} \tag{2}$$

According to the IRR decision criterion, you should *accept* projects in which the IRR is greater than or equalt to an appropriate required rate of return (i) and *reject* projects where the IRR is less than i. The IRR is not an appropriate tool for comparing two projects that are mutually exclusive. Example 4-2 shows how easy it is to compute IRR using a financial calculator.

4-2) Willy Wonka is debating whether to invest in a new Chocolate Gobstopper machine. The project will require an initial investment of $60,000. It is expected to return $10,000/year for the first five years of its life and $8,000/year for the next three. Its scrap value at the end of this time will be $1,000. What is this project's IRR and what should Willy do?

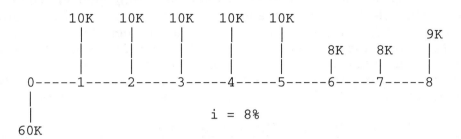

$$\$60{,}000 = \sum_{t=1}^{5} \frac{\$10{,}000}{(1+\text{IRR})^t} + \frac{\$8{,}000}{(1+\text{IRR})^6} + \frac{\$8{,}000}{(1+\text{IRR})^7} + \frac{\$9{,}000}{(1+\text{IRR})^8}$$

HP-10B	EL-733A	BA II Plus
-60,000 $\boxed{\text{CF}_j}$	-60'000 $\boxed{\text{CF}_i}$	$\boxed{\text{CF}}$
10,000 $\boxed{\text{CF}_j}$	5 $\boxed{\text{2ndF}}$ {N$_i$}	$\boxed{\text{2nd}}$ {CLR Work}
5 $\boxed{}$ {N$_j$}	10'000 $\boxed{\text{CF}_i}$	-60,000 $\boxed{\text{ENTER}}$ $\boxed{\downarrow}$
8,000 $\boxed{\text{CF}_j}$	2 $\boxed{\text{2ndF}}$ {N$_i$}	10,000 $\boxed{\text{ENTER}}$ $\boxed{\downarrow}$
2 $\boxed{}$ {N$_j$}	8'000 $\boxed{\text{CF}_i}$	5 $\boxed{\text{ENTER}}$ $\boxed{\downarrow}$
9,000 $\boxed{\text{CF}_j}$	9'000 $\boxed{\text{CF}_i}$	8,000 $\boxed{\text{ENTER}}$ $\boxed{\downarrow}$
8 $\boxed{\text{I/YR}}$	8 $\boxed{\text{i}}$	2 $\boxed{\text{ENTER}}$ $\boxed{\downarrow}$
$\boxed{}$ {IRR/YR} 5.44	$\boxed{\text{IRR}}$ 5.44	9,000 $\boxed{\text{ENTER}}$ $\boxed{\downarrow}$
		1 $\boxed{\text{ENTER}}$ $\boxed{\downarrow}$
		$\boxed{\text{IRR}}$
		$\boxed{\text{CPT}}$ 5.44

Because this investment's IRR of 5.44 percent is less than the firm's cost of capital, Willy should reject the project.

Multiple IRRs

It is possible to come across problems having multiple solutions for the internal rate of return. When this occurs, most financial calculators return an error message. There are not many real-world examples of this sort, however, so it is best to recheck your calculations before concluding that multiple IRRs are involved. Multiple IRRs exist whenever there is an odd number of alternating sign changes in the equation.[2] This may occur in some leasing arrangements and in the "pump problem." Consider an investment in an oil pumping station, which costs $1.5 million at t=0. Revenues of $10 million are received at t=1, but the expense of dismantling the station and cleaning up the environment creates a $10 million loss at t=2. An NPV profile analysis of this project is shown in Figure 4-2.

Figure 4-2. Multiple Internal Rates of Return

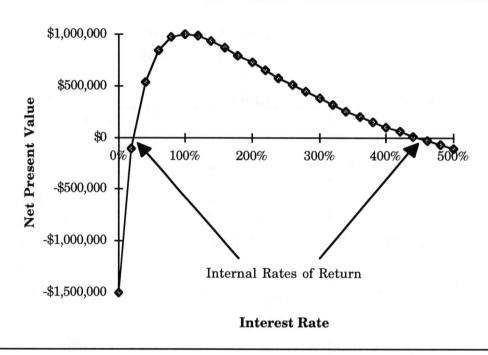

Because there are two possible solutions, your calculator will return an error message. In these situations, it's probably best to use the Net Present Value or Profitability Index decision criteria to evaluate your investment projects.

---

[2]This argument is based on René Descartes' Rule of Signs. Descartes, a noted French philosopher, is perhaps best remembered for *cogito ergo sum* – "I think, therefore I am."

Profitability Index

Another decision criterion relying on discounted cash flows is the Profitability Index (PI), defined as the present value return *per dollar of initial investment*. Most financial calculators do not compute this measure directly, but with a bit of cleverness it's not too difficult to determine. Recall that net present value equals the *difference* between the sum of the discounted future cash flows and the initial investment. The profitability index is the *quotient* of the sum of the discounted future cash flows and the initial investment (Equation 3).

$$PI = \frac{\sum_{t=1}^{n} \frac{CF_t}{(1+i)^t}}{I_0} \tag{3}$$

To compute the PI, first determine the project's net present value using the cash flow registers. Add back the initial outlay to the NPV to get the numerator in Equation 3. Then divide this figure by the initial outlay to arrive at the profitability index. Example 4-3 provides practice in using all three decision-making tools.

4-3) Manjit owns a small electroplating company producing copper-plated snaps and fasteners for the garment trade. Recently, a large clothing manufacturer suggested that he stop producing electroplated goods and focus instead on pure alloys, which create much less pollution during their manufacture. The clothing manufacturer has agreed to purchase Manjit's entire output for the next three years to support this change. Manjit guesses that to retool his entire operation will cost 1,500,000 rupees. Net after-tax cash flows for the next three years are estimated at 400,000, 600,000 and 800,000 rupees, respectively. Manjit has other investment opportunities of similar risk earning 4 percent. Compute the NPV, IRR and PI of this investment.

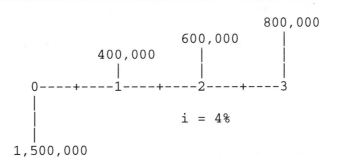

(example continued on next page)

$$\text{NPV} = -\$1,500,000 + \frac{\$400,000}{(1.04)^1} + \frac{\$600,000}{(1.04)^2} + \frac{\$800,000}{(1.04)^3}$$

$$\$1,500,000 = \frac{\$400,000}{(1+\text{IRR})^1} + \frac{\$600,000}{(1+\text{IRR})^2} + \frac{\$800,000}{(1+\text{IRR})^3}$$

HP-10B	EL-733A	BA II Plus
−1,500,000 `CFj`	−1'500'000 `CFi`	`CF`
400,000 `CFj`	400'000 `CFi`	`2nd` {CLR Work}
600,000 `CFj`	600'000 `CFi`	−1,500,000 `ENTER` `↓`
800,000 `CFj`	800'000 `CFi`	400,000 `ENTER` `↓`
4 `I/YR`	4 `i`	1 `ENTER` `↓`
`▢` {NPV} 150,546	`NPV` 150'546	600,000 `ENTER` `↓`
`▢` {IRR/YR} 8.66	`IRR` 8.66	1 `ENTER` `↓`
		800,000 `ENTER` `↓`
		1 `ENTER` `↓`
		`NPV`
		4 `ENTER`
		`↓` `CPT` 150,546
		`IRR` `CPT` 8.66

Net Present Value = 150,546 rupees

Internal Rate of Return = 8.66 percent

Present value of future cash flows = NPV + Initial Outlay

= 150,546 + 1,500,000 = 1,650,546

$$\text{Profitability Index} = \frac{1,650,546}{1,500,000} = 1.10$$

Equivalent Annual Annuity

The equivalent annual annuity (EAA) approach is useful in comparing investment alternatives with different lives.[3] It seeks to find an annual annuity equivalent to each project's net present value calculated over its respective useful life. Essentially, it asks you to solve for the payment (X) in the equation: $NPV = X \cdot PVAF_{(i\%,\, n)}$ where i = the project's hurdle rate and n = the project's useful life. Rearranging terms allows one to express the equivalent annual annuity more directly (Equation 4).

$$\text{Equivalent Annual Annuity} = \frac{\text{Net Present Value}}{\text{PVAF}\,(i\%,\, n)} \qquad (4)$$

The rationale for this method is based upon project replication. One way to analyze projects with different lives is to assume they will be replaced with a series of identical projects *ad infinitum*. In the long run (t=∞), the project chains will have equal lives. One might also think of the equivalent annual annuity as the annual rent one must pay to acquire use of a project. In either case, the larger, or less negative, the equivalent annual annuity, the more desirable the project. Simple NPV analysis is inappropriate for projects with unequal lives because it fails to account for the uneven lengths of the benefit series (or 'disbenefits,' if the future cash flows are *costs*).

A financial calculator makes short work of these calculations. First use the cash flow registers to find the project's NPV and then use this figure as a present value and solve for the unknown payment.

4-4) Oakland Township is considering two proposals for a new sports and recreation complex. The Basic plan has an attractive initial investment and requires substantial maintenance expenditures over its 20-year expected life. The Low Maintenance plan has a higher initial cost but uses more durable materials and consequently will require less care over its 25-year expected life. Either plan will be funded by an issue of municipal bonds at an 8 percent interest rate. Use the equivalent annual annuity method and the information shown below to determine which proposal Oakland Township should adopt.

	Basic Plan	**Low Maintenance**
Initial Outlay	- $375,000	- $475,000
Annual Expenses	- 12,000	- 3,000
Useful Life	20 years	25 years

(example continued on next page)

---

[3]Engineering economists sometimes refer to this approach as the "equivalent uniform annual cost," or EUAC method, because they so frequently deal with costs.

Basic Plan: $\text{NPV} = -\$375{,}000 - \displaystyle\sum_{t=1}^{20} \frac{\$12{,}000}{(1.08)^t} = -\$492{,}818$

HP-10B	EL-733A	BA II Plus
-375,000 [CFj]	-375'000 [CFi]	[CF]
-12,000 [CFj]	20 [2ndF] {Nᵢ}	[2nd] {CLR Work}
20 ☐ {Nⱼ}	-12'000 [CFi]	-375,000 [ENTER] [↓]
8 [I/YR]	8 [i]	-12,000 [ENTER] [↓]
☐ {NPV} -492,818	[NPV] -492'818	20 [ENTER] [↓]
		[NPV]
		8 [ENTER]
		[↓] [CPT] -492,818

$-\$492{,}818 = X \cdot \text{PVAF}_{(8\%,\ 20)}$ Equivalent Annual Annuity = X = $-\$50{,}195$

HP-10B	EL-733A	BA II Plus
492,818 [PV]	492'818 [PV]	492,818 [PV]
20 [N]	20 [n]	20 [N]
8 [I/YR]	8 [i]	8 [I/Y]
[PMT] -50,195	[COMP] [PMT] -50'195	[CPT] [PMT] -50,195

The corresponding figures for the Low Maintenance alternative are:

Low Maintenance: $\text{NPV} = -\$475{,}000 - \displaystyle\sum_{t=1}^{25} \frac{\$3{,}000}{(1.08)^t} = -\$507{,}024$

$-\$507{,}024 = X \cdot \text{PVAF}_{(8\%,\ 25)}$ Equivalent Annual Annuity = X = $-\$47{,}497$

The net present value of the Basic plan is *less* negative than the Low Maintenance plan. However, the latter has a longer useful life. The equivalent annual annuity approach adjusts for this discrepancy and results in a lower annual cost, asuuming both projects are replicated *ad infinitum*. Oakland Township should choose the Low Maintenance proposal (Equivalent Annual Anuity = –$47,497 vs. –$50,195).

Present Value of an Uneven Series of Future Cash Flows

Although the cash flow registers were primarily designed with investment analysis in mind, they can also be used to solve simpler problems such as finding the present value of an uneven series of future cash flows. Recall that the first entry is always the initial outlay (I_0). By letting $I_0 = 0$, it is possible to "fool" the NPV function and quickly determine the present value for *any* series of future cash flows. Example 4-5 shows how to accomplish this using the various calculator models.

4-5) What is the present value of the following series of cash flows? Assume a discount rate of 15 percent. (Note that $CF_0 = \$0$).

$$CF_1 = \$50,000$$
$$CF_2 = \$35,000$$
$$CF_3 - CF_8 = \$20,000$$

```
        50,000
          |          35,000
          |            |        20,000  20,000   ...   20,000
          |            |           |       |             |
  0-------1-------2-------3-------4----  ...  ---8
  |
  PV = ?                         i = 15%
```

$$PV_0 = \frac{\$50,000}{(1.15)^1} + \frac{\$35,000}{(1.15)^2} + \frac{\$20,000}{(1.15)^3} + ... + \frac{\$20,000}{(1.15)^8}$$

(example continued on next page)

HP-10B	EL-733A	BA II Plus
0 [CFj]	0 [CFi]	[CF]
50,000 [CFj]	50'000 [CFi]	[2nd] {CLR Work}
35,000 [CFj]	35'000 [CFi]	0 [ENTER] [↓]
20,000 [CFj]	6 [2ndF] {Ni}	50,000 [ENTER] [↓]
6 [ ] {Nj}	20'000 [CFi]	1 [ENTER] [↓]
15 [I/YR]	15 [i]	35,000 [ENTER] [↓]
[ ] {NPV} 127,176	[NPV] 127'176	1 [ENTER] [↓]
		20,000 [ENTER] [↓]
		6 [ENTER] [↓]
		[NPV]
		15 [ENTER]
		[↓] [CPT] 127,176

The present value of this series of cash flows equals $127,176.

Valuing a Cash Flow Series at Time t ≠ 0

A slight modification of the preceding technique makes it possible to find the value of a cash flow series at *any* point in time. Just calculate the present value of the series in question and then compound this value forward however many periods are necessary. Example 4-6 illustrates this procedure.

4-6) What is the *future* value (i.e., at t=8) of the cash flow series from Example 4-5?

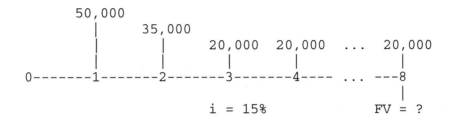

$$FV_8 = \$50{,}000\,(1.15)^7 + \$35{,}000\,(1.15)^6 + \$20{,}000\,(1.15)^5$$
$$+ ... + \$20{,}000\,(1.15)^1 + \$20{,}000$$

or

$$FV = \$127{,}125.54\,(1 + .15)^8$$

$$FV = \$127{,}125.54 \cdot FVIF_{(15\%,\ 8)}$$

HP-10B		EL-733A		BA II Plus	
-127,176	PV	-127'176	PV	-127,176	PV
8	N	8	n	8	N
15	I/YR	15	i	15	I/Y
FV	389,034	COMP FV	389'034	CPT FV	389,034

The future value of the cash flow series from Example 4-5 is $389,034.

Chapter Five

STATISTICS

"There are three kinds of lies – lies, damned lies and statistics."

– Benjamin Disraeli

Much of the field of finance is based upon two human emotions – fear and greed. Stated more formally, financial economists attempt to resolve the impact of an asset's risk and return on human decision-making. At the heart of the matter lie investor preferences, i.e., Is a bird in the hand *really* worth two in the bush? Once a decision has been made concerning these, several elementary statistical techniques are useful in quantifying the exact relationship between risk and return.

Statistics is concerned with the outcome of *events*, or particular states of nature. An event's *probability* reflects the percentage chance of its occurrence. A *probability distribution* is an exhaustive list of all events, together with their associated probabilities of occurrence. Statistical concepts relevant to the introductory finance course include means, standard deviations, correlation coefficients and linear regression. This chapter shows how you can use a financial calculator's statistical functions to estimate expected returns, measures of risk and forecasted values.[1]

Population vs. Sample Statistics

Statistical techniques used in the introductory finance course differ slightly from those encountered in other business disciplines, e.g., operations management and marketing. The chief distinction has to do with the difference between *population* and *sample* statistics. Normally, it is either extremely difficult or very costly to obtain measurements for an entire population. For instance, you might inspect every tenth widget rolling off an assembly line and extrapolate these results to the entire production run. Or we might stand in a particular location surveying passers-by and argue that our sample responses are representative of the population as a whole. Both of these situations involve the use of sample statistics.

Two measures are of general interest: 1) Measures of central tendency, e.g., means, medians and modes and 2) Measures of variation about a given value, e.g., variances and standard deviations. If you have data on all members of a population and each event has an equal probability of occurrence, the mean and standard deviation are defined as:

---

[1]It is by no means intended as a complete survey of the field. Please refer to a statistics textbook or your user manual for more detailed information.

$$\mu = \frac{\displaystyle\sum_{i=1}^{n} x_i}{n} \tag{1}$$

$$\sigma = \sqrt{\frac{\displaystyle\sum_{i=1}^{n} (x_i - \mu)^2}{n}} \tag{2}$$

where: μ = population mean
σ = population standard deviation
n = number of outcomes or events
x_i = ith outcome of event x

In business, information on a complete population is the exception, rather than the rule. Corresponding sample statistics have been developed which do a good job of estimating population parameters when the probability distribution is known. For populations believed to be *normally distributed*, the sample mean and sample standard deviation are:

$$E(x) = \bar{x} = \frac{\displaystyle\sum_{i=1}^{n} x_i}{n} \tag{3}$$

$$s = \sqrt{\frac{\displaystyle\sum_{i=1}^{n} (x_i - \bar{x})^2}{n-1}} \tag{4}$$

where: $\bar{x}$ = sample mean
s = sample standard deviation

The HP-10B, EL-733A and BA II Plus are capable of computing means and standard deviations for complete and sample populations. Their use is illustrated in Examples 5-1 and 5-2.

5-1) The Hiawatha Transport Company maintains a fleet of nine delivery trucks in varying ages and states of repair. The firm's Chief Financial Officer is investigating the fleet's fuel use with an eye towards replacing some of the less-efficient vehicles. The following data is representative of a typical month. How fuel-efficient is the "average" truck? What is the standard deviation around this estimate?

(example continued on next page)

Truck	Distance	Fuel Use	Fuel Efficiency
1	810 km	128 l	6.3 km/l
2	350	47	7.4
3	1450	201	7.2
4	1240	133	9.3
5	770	143	5.4
6	560	86	6.5
7	1130	111	10.2
8	930	160	5.8
9	880	160	5.5

HP-10B	EL-733A	BA II Plus
		[2nd] {Data}
	[2ndF] {MODE}	[2nd] {CLR Work}
6.3 [Σ+]	6.3 [DATA] *	6.3 [ENTER] [↓] [↓]
7.4 [Σ+]	7.4 [DATA]	7.4 [ENTER] [↓] [↓]
7.2 [Σ+]	7.2 [DATA]	7.2 [ENTER] [↓] [↓]
9.3 [Σ+]	9.3 [DATA]	9.3 [ENTER] [↓] [↓]
5.4 [Σ+]	5.4 [DATA]	5.4 [ENTER] [↓] [↓]
6.5 [Σ+]	6.5 [DATA]	6.5 [ENTER] [↓] [↓]
10.2 [Σ+]	10.2 [DATA]	10.2 [ENTER] [↓] [↓]
5.8 [Σ+]	5.8 [DATA]	5.8 [ENTER] [↓] [↓]
5.5 [Σ+]	5.5 [DATA]	5.5 [ENTER] [↓] [↓]
☐ {$\bar{x}, \bar{y}$} 7.07	[2ndF] {$\bar{x}$} 7.07	[2nd] {Stat}
☐ {σx, σy} 1.59	[2ndF] {σx} 1.59	[2nd] (SET} **
		[↓] [↓] 7.07
		[↓] [↓] 1.59

* The [M+] key becomes the [DATA] key in Statistics mode.

** Continue pressing [2nd] {SET} until "1–V" is displayed for one-variable statistics.

Because we have data on the entire fleet, the appropriate statistical measures are those based on populations. The population mean fuel efficiency is 7.07 km/liter (approximately 16.7 miles/gallon). The population standard deviation is 1.59 km/liter (approximately 3.74 miles/gallon).

5-2) The Earlysville Country Store allows its customers a limited amount of credit purchases. Pam Anderson, the store's owner, is concerned about possible abuse of these privileges. She has pulled twenty credit slips at random from the pickle barrel she uses as a filing cabinet to verify her suspicions. Use the data shown below to estimate the average amount of outstanding credit per customer and the standard deviation of this estimate.

Customer	Credit	Customer	Credit
1	$100	11	$225
2	$140	12	$160
3	$180	13	$258
4	$ 70	14	$120
5	$140	15	$ 55
6	$157	16	$ 25
7	$345	17	$160
8	$ 92	18	$100
9	$150	19	$140
10	$125	20	$ 20

HP-10B	EL-733A	BA II Plus
		[2nd] {Data}
	[2ndF] {MODE}	[2nd] {CLR Work}
100 [Σ+]	100 [DATA] *	100 [ENTER] [↓] [↓]
140 [Σ+]	140 [DATA]	140 [ENTER] [↓] [↓]
180 [Σ+]	180 [DATA]	180 [ENTER] [↓] [↓]
etc.	etc.	etc.
20 [Σ+]	20 [DATA]	20 [ENTER] [↓] [↓]
[ ] {x̄,ȳ} 138.10	[2ndF] {x̄} 138.10	[2nd] {Stat}
[ ] {Sx,Sy} 76.70	[2ndF] {sx} 76.70	[2nd] {SET}**
		[↓] [↓] 138.10
		[↓] 76.70

* The [M+] key becomes the [DATA] key in Statistics mode.

** Continue pressing [2nd] {SET} until "1–V" is displayed for one-variable statistics.

The sample mean equals $138.10. The sample standard deviation is $76.70.

Correcting Errors

Everyone makes mistakes entering long lists of data. Fortunately, each calculator model provides some method of correcting wrong entries without having to clear and re-enter the entire data series. To delete an entry on the HP-10B, key in the value and press ☐{Σ-}. This removes the offending data point and allows you to re-enter it correctly. A similar procedure applies to the EL-733A. In Statistics mode, re-enter the incorrect entry and press the [CD], or "Change Data" key. Enter the correct number and press the [DATA] key to complete the switch.

Because the BA II Plus stores statistical data in list form, it is possible to scroll back and review previous entries using the arrow keys. This makes it much easier to spot errors in the data. If you find an incorrect entry, press [2nd]{DEL} to delete it. To re-insert the correct value, press [2nd]{INS}, key in a new x-value and press [ENTER].

Weighted Averages

Often events are not equally probable. This is particularly true for security returns; certain outcomes are much more likely to occur. In many instant lottery games, for instance, several outcomes are possible – you may win a specified sum ($10, $25, $100, etc.) or "lose" the cost of the ticket itself.

Weighted averages provide a method of accounting for differences in the likelihood of an event's occurrence. The expected value, or most likely outcome, is:

$$E(x) = \bar{x} = \sum_{i=1}^{n} \alpha_i \cdot x_i \tag{5}$$

where: $E(x)$ = expected value of event x; aka "mean" value
           α_i = probability of the ith outcome occurring
           x_i = ith outcome of event x

Probability distributions can be constructed for almost any "uncertain" event.[2] In finance, weighted averages are sometimes used to determine an asset's most likely return, or expected value. An asset's *expected return* is calculated as the weighted mean of all possible returns, where the weights are determined by the associated probabilities of occurrence. To compute an expected value, multiply each possible outcome (x_i) by its associated probability of occurrence (α_i) and sum the resulting products. This process insures that higher-probability outcomes will "count" more than lower-probability outcomes. Example 5-3 illustrates the computation of weighted means.

---

[2]Technically, *uncertainty* refers to variability in outcomes while *risk* requires the decisionmaker be able to estimate probabilities. Once probabilities are assigned, it is possible to value or price risk. Uncertainty, however, cannot be valued.

5-3) Matt and Janet have determined the following probability distribution of returns for a security whose performance is highly correlated with the state of the US economy. What is this security's expected return?

Economy	Probability	Return
Overheating	.05	25 %
Expansion	.15	15 %
"Normal"	.50	10 %
Recession	.20	5 %
Depression	.10	- 5 %

$$E(x) = .05(25) + .15(15) + .50(10) + .20(5) + .10(-5)$$

$$E(x) = 9.00 = 9 \text{ percent}$$

Hewlett-Packard HP-10B	Sharp EL-733A*
25.00 INPUT 0.05 Σ+	25.00 (x,y) × 0.05 DATA
15.00 INPUT 0.15 Σ+	15.00 (x,y) × 0.15 DATA
10.00 INPUT 0.50 Σ+	10.00 (x,y) × 0.50 DATA
5.00 INPUT 0.20 Σ+	5.00 (x,y) × 0.20 DATA
-5.00 INPUT 0.10 Σ+	-5.00 (x,y) × 0.10 DATA
☐ {x̄w} 9.00	2ndF {x̄} 9.00

* In Statistics mode, the M+ key becomes the DATA key and the RM key becomes the (x,y) key.

(example continued on next page)

Texas Instruments BA II Plus

$\boxed{\text{2nd}}$ {Data} $\boxed{\text{2nd}}$ {CLR Work}

25.00 $\boxed{\text{ENTER}}$ $\boxed{\downarrow}$ 5.00* $\boxed{\text{ENTER}}$ $\boxed{\downarrow}$

15.00 $\boxed{\text{ENTER}}$ $\boxed{\downarrow}$ 15.00 $\boxed{\text{ENTER}}$ $\boxed{\downarrow}$

10.00 $\boxed{\text{ENTER}}$ $\boxed{\downarrow}$ 50.00 $\boxed{\text{ENTER}}$ $\boxed{\downarrow}$

5.00 $\boxed{\text{ENTER}}$ $\boxed{\downarrow}$ 20.00 $\boxed{\text{ENTER}}$ $\boxed{\downarrow}$

−5.00 $\boxed{\text{ENTER}}$ $\boxed{\downarrow}$ 10.00 $\boxed{\text{ENTER}}$ $\boxed{\downarrow}$

$\boxed{\text{2nd}}$ {Stat} $\boxed{\text{2nd}}$ {CLR Work}

$\boxed{\text{2nd}}$ {SET}   ** *Press until "1-V" is displayed*

$\boxed{\downarrow}$ $\boxed{\downarrow}$ 9.00

* When computing weighted averages, the BA II Plus requires all "weights" to be entered as whole numbers, NOT as decimal fractions.

This security has an expected return of 9.00 percent.

Weighted averages are used in determining portfolio returns, portfolio betas and the *weighted-average cost of capital* (Example 5-4).

5-4) Kretzbacher Company has only three types of outstanding securities; bonds, preferred and common stock, and no current liabilities. Investors require an after-tax yield of 9 percent on the firm's long-term bonds, 13 percent on its preferred stock and 16 percent on common stock. Kretzbacher believes its optimal capital structure to be 35% debt, 15% preferred equity and 50% common equity. Compute Kretzbacher's weighted-average cost of capital, assuming new investors will require returns greater or equal to those required by current investors.

WACC = .35(9) + .15(13) + .50(16) = 13.10 percent

Hewlett-Packard HP-10B	Sharp EL-733A
9.00 INPUT 0.35 $\Sigma+$	9.00 (x,y) × 0.35 DATA
13.00 INPUT 0.15 $\Sigma+$	13.00 (x,y) × 0.15 DATA
16.00 INPUT 0.50 $\Sigma+$	16.00 (x,y) × 0.50 DATA
☐ {x̄w} 13.10	2ndF {x̄} 13.10

Texas Instruments BA II Plus

2nd {Data} 2nd {CLR Work}

9.00 ENTER ↓ 35.00* ENTER ↓

13.00 ENTER ↓ 15.00 ENTER ↓

16.00 ENTER ↓ 50.00 ENTER ↓

2nd {Stat} 2nd {CLR Work}

2nd {SET} ** *Press until "1-V" is displayed*

↓ ↓ 13.10

* When computing weighted averages, the BA II Plus requires all "weights" to be entered as whole numbers, NOT as decimal fractions.

Kretzbacher's weighted-average cost of capital equals 13.10 percent.

Linear Regression

Regression analysis is a powerful tool used in many business disciplines. It is useful in determining the degree of association between two sets of data. As its name implies, *linear* regression assumes a straight-line relationship. The most common regression technique, ordinary least squares (OLS), estimates a line's slope and intercept coefficients by minimizing the sum of the observations' squared deviations from the line of best fit where:

$$y = mx + b \qquad\qquad (6a)$$

$$m = \frac{\sum xy - \dfrac{\sum x \sum y}{n}}{\sum x^2 - \dfrac{(\sum x)^2}{n}} \qquad\qquad (6b)$$

$$b = \bar{y} - m\bar{x} \qquad\qquad (6c)$$

and

y = dependent variable	$\bar{y}$ = mean of y-values
x = independent variable	$\bar{x}$ = mean of x-values
m = slope coefficient	n = number of observations
b = intercept coefficient	

Regression notation is not well-standardized, and it is important to understand the symbols used by *your* model of financial calculator. Both the BA II Plus and the EL-733A write the equation for a line as: y = bx + a, where b is the slope and a is the intercept.

The correlation coefficient (r) describes the degree to which two variables are related. Squaring the correlation coefficient gives the *coefficient of detemination* (r^2), which measures how well the "line of best fit" fits. Both are useful in establishing the general validity of a relationship.[3]

Two forms of regression are commonly found in the introductory finance course: cross-sectional and time-series analysis. In cross-sectional analysis, a distribution of outcomes is examined at a single point in time, while time-series analysis investigates behavior across time. Both types are illustrated in Examples 5-5 through 5-7.

---

[3]All three calculator models also report intermediate sums of squares, should you be interested in constructing your own statistical measures.

5-5) Schildkröte Detergents markets a variety of cleaning agents in various package sizes. Data for one particular product, "Clean-All," is shown below. What is the relationship between Gross Margin (y) and Package Size (x)? On the basis of this information, what would you anticipate the gross margin on a new 1500 ml package to be?

(x) Package Size	(y) Gross Margin
============	============
300 ml	35 %
500 ml	40 %
750 ml	35 %
1000 ml	20 %
2000 ml	30 %
5000 ml	20 %

(example continued on next page)

Hewlett-Packard HP-10B

```
    300 [INPUT]  35 [Σ+]
    500 [INPUT]  40 [Σ+]
    750 [INPUT]  35 [Σ+]
  1,000 [INPUT]  20 [Σ+]
  2,000 [INPUT]  30 [Σ+]
  5,000 [INPUT]  20 [Σ+]
        0 [ ] {ŷ,m}     35.04   <== y-intercept
          [ ] {SWAP}    -0.003  <== slope
 [ ] {x̂,r} [ ] {SWAP}  -0.67   <== corr. coefficient
    1,500 [ ] {ŷ,m}     30.29   <== predicted y
```

Sharp EL-733A

```
            [2ndF] {MODE}
    300 [(x,y)] * 35 [DATA]
    500 [(x,y)]   40 [DATA]
    750 [(x,y)]   35 [DATA]
  1'000 [(x,y)]   20 [DATA]
  2'000 [(x,y)]   30 [DATA]
  5'000 [(x,y)]   20 [DATA]
          [2ndF] {a}    35.04   <== y-intercept
          [2ndF] {b}    -0.003  <== slope
          [2ndF] {r}    -0.67   <== corr. coefficient
  1'500 [2ndF] {y'}     30.29   <== predicted y
```

* In Statistics mode, the [M+] key becomes the [DATA] key
and the [RM] key becomes the [(x,y)] key.

(example continued on next page)

2nd {Data} 2nd {CLR Work}

300 ENTER ↓ 35 ENTER ↓

500 ENTER ↓ 40 ENTER ↓

750 ENTER ↓ 35 ENTER ↓

1,000 ENTER ↓ 20 ENTER ↓

2,000 ENTER ↓ 30 ENTER ↓

5,000 ENTER ↓ 20 ENTER ↓

2nd {Stat} 2nd {CLR Work}

↓ ↓ ↓ ↓

↓ ↓ ↓ ↓ 35.04 <== y-intercept (a)

↓ -0.003 <== slope (b)

↓ -0.67 <== corr. coefficient

↓ 1,500 ENTER

↓ CPT 30.29 <== predicted y

The relationship between Package Size (x) and Gross Margin (y) is:

$$y = 35.04 - 0.003x \qquad r^2 = (-0.67)^2 = 0.45$$

According to these results, you would anticipate a 1500-ml package to carry a gross margin of 30.29 percent. However, the low value for r^2 raises concerns about the validity of assuming a linear relationship between package size and gross margin.

5-6) Rick's Aeronautic Supplies has the following 5-year sales history. Use linear regression to forecast expected sales for the next three years.

x	Year	Sales
1	1987	88,000
2	1989	101,000
3	1990	111,000
4	1991	115,000
5	1992	121,000

Hewlett-Packard HP-10B

1 [INPUT] 88,000 [Σ+]

2 [INPUT] 101,000 [Σ+]

3 [INPUT] 111,000 [Σ+]

4 [INPUT] 115,000 [Σ+]

5 [INPUT] 121,000 [Σ+]

0 ☐ {$\hat{y}$,m}   83,200   <== y-intercept

☐ {SWAP}   8,000   <== slope

6 ☐ {$\hat{y}$,m}   131,200   <== predicted y

7 ☐ {$\hat{y}$,m}   139,200   <== predicted y

8 ☐ {$\hat{y}$,m}   147,200   <== predicted y

(example continued on next page)

Sharp EL-733A

2ndF {MODE}

1 (x,y)   88'000 DATA

2 (x,y)   101'000 DATA

3 (x,y)   111'000 DATA

4 (x,y)   115'000 DATA

5 (x,y)   121'000 DATA

                  2ndF {a}   83'200 <== y-intercept

                  2ndF {b}   8'000 <== slope

        6   2ndF {y'}   131'200 <== predicted y

        7   2ndF {y'}   139'200 <== predicted y

        8   2ndF {y'}   147'200 <== predicted y

Texas Instruments BA II Plus

2nd {Data} 2nd {CLR Work}

1 ENTER ↓   88,000 ENTER ↓

2 ENTER ↓   101,000 ENTER ↓

3 ENTER ↓   111,000 ENTER ↓

4 ENTER ↓   115,000 ENTER ↓

5 ENTER ↓   121,000 ENTER ↓

   2nd {Stat} 2nd {CLR Work}

                  ↓ ↓ ↓ ↓

                  ↓ ↓ ↓ ↓   83,200 <== y-intercept (a)

                           ↓   8,000 <== slope (b)

  ↓ ↓   6   ENTER ↓ CPT   131,200 <== predicted y

     ↑   7   ENTER ↓ CPT   139,200 <== predicted y

     ↑   8   ENTER ↓ CPT   147,200 <== predicted y

5-7) A security's beta coefficient can be estimated by using a simple linear regression model. The *characteristic line* is obtained by regressing a time series of historical security returns against returns on the market portfolio. Beta equals the line's slope. What is the beta coefficient for the security whose returns are depicted below?[4]

Market Return (x)	Security Return (y)
4.594	-1.687
7.497	-2.994
-9.255	-17.447
9.317	-4.779
8.632	13.333
3.072	11.064
-0.271	0.615
-5.034	-3.715
0.030	20.013
12.952	23.899

Hewlett-Packard HP-10B

4.594 [INPUT]   -1.687 [Σ+]

7.497 [INPUT]   -2.994 [Σ+]

-9.255 [INPUT]   -17.447 [Σ+]

9.317 [INPUT]   -4.779 [Σ+]

8.632 [INPUT]   13.333 [Σ+]

3.072 [INPUT]   11.064 [Σ+]

-0.271 [INPUT]   0.615 [Σ+]

-5.034 [INPUT]   -3.715 [Σ+]

0.030 [INPUT]   20.013 [Σ+]

12.952 [INPUT]   23.899 [Σ+]

0 ☐ {ŷ,m}   0.5568 <== y-intercept

☐ {SWAP}   1.0381 <== slope (= beta)

(example continued on next page)

---

[4]The "standard" method for estimating beta coefficients uses five years of monthly returns, i.e., 60 data points.

Sharp EL-733A

2ndF {MODE}

4.594 (x,y)   -1.687 DATA
7.497 (x,y)   -2.994 DATA
-9.255 (x,y) -17.447 DATA
9.317 (x,y)   -4.779 DATA
8.632 (x,y)   13.333 DATA
3.072 (x,y)   11.064 DATA
-0.271 (x,y)   0.615 DATA
-5.034 (x,y) -3.715 DATA
0.030 (x,y)   20.013 DATA
12.952 (x,y) 23.899 DATA

2ndF {a} 0.5568 <== y-intercept

2ndF {b} 1.0381 <== slope (= beta)

Texas Instruments BA II Plus

2nd {Data} 2nd {CLR Work}

4.594 ENTER ↓   -1.687 ENTER ↓
7.497 ENTER ↓   -2.994 ENTER ↓
-9.255 ENTER ↓ -17.447 ENTER ↓
9.317 ENTER ↓   -4.779 ENTER ↓
8.632 ENTER ↓   13.333 ENTER ↓
3.072 ENTER ↓   11.064 ENTER ↓
-0.271 ENTER ↓   0.615 ENTER ↓
-5.034 ENTER ↓ -3.715 ENTER ↓
0.030 ENTER ↓   20.013 ENTER ↓
12.952 ENTER ↓ 23.899 ENTER ↓

2nd {Stat} 2nd {CLR Work}

↓ ↓ ↓ ↓

↓ ↓ ↓ ↓ 0.5568 <== y-intercept (a)

↓ 1.0381 <== slope (b = beta)

Chapter Six

ADDITIONAL PROBLEMS

"The end of learning is gracious living."

– Inscription on Mary Trowbridge House
Kalamazoo College
Kalamazoo, Michigan

This chapter contains sixty problems providing additional practice in financial analysis. Some problems have been taken from other texts. These are identified using the following key:

BH	Block, Stanley B. and Geoffrey A. Hirt, *Foundations of Financial Management*, 9th Ed., (Burr Ridge, IL: Irwin/McGraw-Hill, 2000).
BMM	Brealey, Richard A., Myers, Stewart C. and Alan J. Marcus, *Fundamentals of Corporate Finance*, 2nd Ed. (Burr Ridge, IL: Irwin/McGraw-Hill, 1999).
RWJ Essentials	Ross, Stephen A., Westerfield, Randolph W. and Bradford D. Jordan, *Essentials of Corporate Finance*, 2nd Ed. (Burr Ridge, IL: Irwin/McGraw-Hill, 1999).
RWJ Fundamentals	Ross, Stephen A., Westerfield, Randolph W. and Bradford D. Jordan, *Fundamentals of Corporate Finance*, 5th Ed., (Burr Ridge, IL: Irwin/McGraw-Hill, 2000).

1. Determine the Future Value Interest Factor (FVIF) for six periods at 4 percent. Find the Present Value Annuity Factor (PVAF) for 30 periods at 6.5 percent.

2. The noted author Edgar Allan Poe entered the University of Virginia as a student in 1826. He was forced to leave one year later, partially due to his inability to pay off $2,000 worth of gambling debts. Assuming an annual interest rate of 5 percent, how much money would you need to square his accounts in 2000, 173 years later?

3. Rarely Prudent, Inc., has an unfunded pension liability of $425 million that must be paid in 23 years. To assess the value of the firm's stock, financial analysts want to discount this liability back to the present. If the relevant discount rate is 7.5 percent, what is the present value of the liability? (RWJ Essentials, p. 105, #10)

4. If you deposit $1,000 at the end of each year for the next 15 years into an account paying 8.5 percent interest, how much money will you have in the account in 15 years? How much will you have in 45 years? (RWJ Essentials, p. 137, #6)

5. The original Barbie doll was introduced in 1959 at a price of $2.99. In March 1998, collectors were willing to pay $8,300 for a mint-condition doll in its original box. What was the average annual rate of return on this 'investment'?

6. A famous quarterback just signed a $15 million contract providing $3 million a year for 5 years. A less famous receiver signed a $14 million 5-year contract providing $4 million now and $2 million a year for 5 years. Who is better paid? The interest rate is 12 percent. (BMM, p. 93, #17)

7. Tom has just been given a "golden handshake" – the opportunity to take early retirement at age 55. He may choose to receive his pension either as a $550,000 lump sum or in monthly payments of $5,000 for the rest of his life. In making this choice, a key consideration is when Tom expects to depart this mortal world. Assuming an annual discount rate of 9 percent, at what life expectancy is Tom indifferent between the two alternatives?

8. Congratulations! You've just won the $20 million first prize in the Subscriptions R Us Sweepstakes. Unfortunately, the sweepstakes will actually give you the $20 million in $500,000 annual installments over the next 40 years, beginning next year. If your appropriate discount rate is 12 percent per year, how much money did you really win? (RWJ Fundamentals, p. 174, #48)

9. Al Rosen invests $25,000 in a mint condition 1952 Mickey Mantle baseball card. He expects the card to increase in value 12 percent a year for the next 10 years. How much will his card be worth after 10 years? (BH, p. 260, #10)

10. On January 1, 1997, Mike Irwin, Jr. bought 100 shares of stock at $14 per share. On December 31, 1999, he sold the stock for $21 per share. What is his annual rate of return? (BH, p. 262, #57)

11. In his autobiography, former Chrysler CEO Lee Iacocca recounted an innovative financing ploy he developed to increase sales of Ford cars during the early part of his career in the automotive industry. Entitled "56 for '56," it allowed customers to purchase a new 1956 model for a 10 percent down payment, followed by three years of monthly payments of $56. Suppose you bought a new Ford costing $2,050. What was the implied annual interest rate on this purchase?

12. You want to lease a new sports car from Muscle Motors for $42,000. The lease contract is in the form of a 48-month annuity due at a 10.5 percent annual percentage rate. What will your monthly lease payments be? (RWJ Fundamentals, p. 186, #157)

13. You've just joined the investment banking firm of Godel, Esher, and Bock. They've offered you two different salary arrangements. You can have $50,000 per year for the next two years or $35,000 per year for the next two years, along with a $30,000 signing bonus today. If the interest rate is 12 percent compounded monthly, which do you prefer? (RWJ Essentials, p. 139, #25)

14. Last National Bank charges 7.5 percent, compounded quarterly, on its business loans. Last United Bank charges 10 percent, compounded semiannually. As a potential borrower, which bank would you go to for a new loan? (RWJ Essentials, p. 138, #14)

15. Inflation in Brazil in 1992 averaged about 23 percent per month. What was the annual inflation rate? (BMM, p. 97, #61)

16. If you take out an $8,000 car loan that calls for 48 monthly payments at an annual percentage rate of 10 percent, what is your monthly payment? What is the effective annual interest rate on the loan? (BMM, p. 93, #18)

17. Your Christmas ski vacation was great, but unfortunately it ran a bit over budget. All is not lost, because you just received an offer in the mail to transfer your $10,000 balance from your current credit card, which charges an annual rate of 11.9 percent, to a new credit card charging a rate of 5.9 percent. How much faster could you pay the loan off by making your planned monthly payments of $200 with the new card? What if there was a 2 percent fee charged on any balances transferred? (RWJ Fundamentals, p. 177, #67)

18. Romulus Bank offers a two-year $10,000 Certificate of Deposit (CD) at an interest rate of 12 percent, compounded *annually*. Remus Bank has a two-year $10,000 CD that compounds interest on a *quarterly* basis. What *nominal* rate of interest must Remus Bank offer in order for you to be indifferent between the two investments? *Note:* Both CDs have the same level of risk.

19. Morgan Jennings, a geography professor, invests $50,000 in a piece of land that is expected to increase in value by 12 percent per year for the next five years. He will take the proceeds and provide himself with a 10-year annuity. Assuming a 12 percent interest rate, how much will this annuity be? (BH, p. 262, #25)

20. Odysseus is planning a voyage in which he will visit the Portal of Hades, hear the song of the Sirens, battle Neptune, and live with the lovely goddess Circe. Alas, this can not continue forever. Odysseus knows that he must eventually return to Ithaca, settle down, and lead the domestic life. At retirement, Odysseus would like to be able to withdraw 50,000 drachmas a year, every year, until he exhausts his savings. Today is Odysseus' 25th birthday. Assume he deposits 2,366 drachmas into an account at the end of this and every year for the next 30 years. Further assume that the account pays interest at a 10 percent annual rate. Odysseus plans to retire on his 55th birthday, at which time he will start making the 50,000 drachma withdrawals mentioned above (i.e., the *first* withdrawal begins at t=55). How old will Odysseus be when he makes his **last** withdrawal?

21. You are chairperson of the investment fund for the Eastern Football League. You are asked to set up a fund of semiannual payments to be compounded semiannually to accumulate a sum of $100,000 after ten years at an 8 percent annual rate (20 payments). The first payment into the fund is to occur six months from today, and the last payment is to take place at the end of the tenth year. Determine how much the semiannual payment should be. (Round to whole numbers.)

    On the day after the fourth payment is made (the beginning of the third year) the interest rate goes up to a 10 percent annual rate, and you can earn a 10 percent annual rate on funds that have been accumulated as well as all future payments into the fund. Interest is to be compounded semiannually on all funds. Determine how much the revised semiannual payments should be after this rate change (there are 16 payments and compounding dates). The next payment will be in the middle of the third year. (Round all values to whole numbers,) (BH, p. 263, #32)

22. Your younger sister, Linda, will start college in five years. She has just informed your parents that she wants to go to Hampton University, which will cost $17,000 per year for four years (cost assumed to come at the end of each year). Anticipating Linda's ambitions, your parents started investing $2,000 per year five years ago and will continue to do so for five more years. How much more will your parents have to invest each year for the next five years to have the necessary funds for Linda's education? Use 10 percent as the appropriate interest rate throughout this problem (for discounting or compounding). (BH, p. 263, #33)

23. When Marilyn Monroe died on August 5, 1962, her once-husband Joe DiMaggio arranged to have a fresh red rose placed on her grave every day in perpetuity. If roses were selling for 50¢ at that time and the annual rate of interest was 5 percent, how much should "Joltin' Joe" have paid the florist?

24. The preferred stock of Ultra Corporation pays an annual dividend of $6.30. It has a required rate of return of 9 percent. Compute the price of the preferred stock. (BH, p. 293, #15)

25. What is the value of an investment that pays $6,500 every *other* year forever, if the first payment occurs one year from today and the discount rate is 16 percent compounded daily? What is the value today if the first payment occurs four years from today? (RWJ Fundamentals, p. 178, #72)

26. You believe that the Non-Stick Gum Factory will pay a dividend of $2 on its common stock next year. Thereafter, you expect dividends to grow at a rate of 6 percent a year in perpetuity. If you require a return of 12 percent on your investment, how much should you be prepared to pay for the stock? (BMM, p. 139, #27)

27. A firm pays a $4.90 dividend at the end of year one (D_1), has a stock price of $70, and a constant growth rate (g) of 6 percent. Compute the required rate of return (k_e). (BH, p. 294, #23)

28. A General Motors bond carries a coupon rate of 8 percent, has 9 years until maturity, and sells at a yield to maturity of 9 percent. What interest payments do bondholders receive each year? At what price does the bond sell? (Assume annual interest payments). What will happen to the bond price if the yield to maturity falls to 7 percent? (BMM, p. 137, #9)

29. Robert Brown III is considering a bond investment in Southwest Technology. The $1,000 par value bonds have a quoted annual interest rate of 8 percent and interest is paid semiannually. The yield to maturity on the bonds is 10 percent annual interest. There are 25 years to maturity. Compute the price of the bonds based on semiannual analysis. (BH, p. 292, #13)

30. Merton Enterprises has bonds on the market making annual payments, with 13 years to maturity, and selling for $825. At this price, the bonds yield 7 percent. What must the coupon rate be on Merton's bonds? (RWJ Essentials, p. 176, #5)

31. BDJ Co. wants to issue new 15-year bonds for some much-needed expansion projects. The company currently has 9 percent coupon bonds on the market that sell for $921.69, make semiannual payments, and mature in 15 years. What coupon rate should the company set on its new bonds if it wants them to sell at par? (RWJ Essentials, p. 177, #16)

32. You buy an 8 percent coupon, 10-year maturity bond for $980. A year later, the bond price is $1,050. [The bond pays interest semiannually]. What is the new yield to maturity on the bond? What is your rate of return over the year? (BMM, p. 138, #15)

33. The Back Street Girls Corporation has two different bonds currently outstanding. Bond M has a face value of $20,000 and matures in 20 years. The bond makes no payments for the first six years, then pays $1,000 semiannually over the subsequent eight years, and finally pays $1,750 semiannually over the last six years. Bond N also has a face value of $20,000 and a maturity of 20 years; it makes no coupon payments over the life of the bond. If the required return on both these bonds is 14 percent compounded semiannually, what is the current price of Bond M? Of Bond N? (RWJ Fundamentals, p. 216, #28)

34. J. P. Goop wishes to borrow $5,000 against the accumulated cash value of his life insurance policy to consolidate his outstanding credit card debts. The loan requires amortizing *quarterly* payments of principal and interest at an 8 percent annual rate over a 5-year term. What is the amount of his quarterly payments? What portion of the ***third*** payment represents repayment of principal? How much interest will he have paid at the end of the first ***year***?

35. Mike and Marilyn just bought their first home for $125,000. In order to pay for their purchase, they took out a $100,000 mortgage loan requiring monthly payments of $804.62 for 30 years. What will the outstanding balance on their loan be after ten years? After twenty years?

36. Home loans typically involve "points," which are fees charged by the lender. Each point charged means that the borrower must pay 1 percent of the loan amount as a fee. For example, if the loan is for $100,000, and two points are charged, the loan repayment schedule is calculated on a $100,000 loan, but the net amount the borrower receives is only $98,000. What is the effective annual interest rate charged on such a loan assuming loan repayment occurs over 360 months? Assume the interest rate is 1 percent per month. (BMM, p. 95, #40)

37. You need a 30-year, fixed-rate mortgage to buy a new home for $200,000. Your mortgage bank will lend you the money at a 6.5 percent annual percentage rate (APR) for this 360-month loan. However, you can only afford monthly payments of $1,000, so you offer to pay off any remaining loan balance at the end of the loan in the form of a single balloon payment. How large will this balloon payment have to be for you to keep your monthly payments at $1,000? (RWJ Fundamentals, p. 174, #42)

38. In the 1994 NBA draft, no one was surprised when the Milwaukee Bucks took Glenn "Big Dog" Robinson with the first pick, but Robinson wanted big bucks from the Bucks: a 13-year deal worth a total of $100 million. He had to settle for $68 million over 10 years. His contract called for $2.9 million the first year, with annual raises of $870,000. How big a bite did the Big Dog take, assuming a discount rate of 12 percent? (RWJ Fundamentals, p. 174, #43)

39. Your favorite security broker left a message on your answering machine last evening to the effect that "... 3-year FizzBuzzes are a particularly good buy at an annual yield of 8 percent ..." You recall that FizzBuzzes are contracts which specify payments of $50 at the end of **odd** half-year periods and $70 at the end of **even** half-year periods. Using an annual discount rate of 8 percent, what is the most one should pay for a three-year (i.e. 6-payment) FizzBuzz?

40. ABC Co. has identified an investment project with the following cash flows.

Year	Cash Flow
====	=========
1	$ 500
2	600
3	700
4	800

If the discount rate is 7 percent, what is the future value of these cash flows in year 4? What is the future value at a discount rate of 10 percent? At 22 percent? (RWJ Essentials, p. 137, #2)

41. An investment has an installed cost of $243,715. The cash flows over the four-year life of the investment are projected to be $75,429, $153,408, $102,389, and $45,000. If the discount rate is zero, what is the net present value (NPV)? If the discount rate is infinite, what is the NPV? At what discount rate is the NPV just equal to zero? (RWJ Essentials, p. 230, #15)

42. Widespread concern about global warming has led the citizens of Lilliput to reconsider construction of a nuclear power plant, which does not emit carbon dioxide, one of the major "greenhouse gases." The plant is estimated to cost $4.5 million and is expected to yield $2.8 million in annual after-tax cash flows over its 40-year useful life. $10 million in decommissioning costs are projected at the end of this period. Determine the net present value, profitability index, and equivalent annual annuity of this project assuming an interest rate of 18 percent.

43. Aerospace Dynamics will invest $110,000 in a project that will produce the following cash flows. The cost of capital is 11 percent. Should the project be undertaken? (BH, p. 371, #9)

Year	Cash Flow
====	=========
1	$ 36,000
2	44,000
3	38,000
4	- 44,000
5	81,000

44. The Ott Group, Inc., has identified the following two mutually exclusive projects:

Year	Project 1	Project 2
====	=========	=========
0	- $12,500	- $12,500
1	4,000	1,000
2	5,000	6,000
3	6,000	5,000
4	1,000	4,000

What is the internal rate of return (IRR) for each of these projects? If you apply the IRR decision rule, which project should the company accept? Is this decision necessarily correct? If the required return is 11 percent, what is the net present value (NPV) for each of these projects? Which project will you choose if you apply the NPV decision rule? (RWJ Essentials, p. 229, #10)

45. Dixie Dynamite Company is evaluating two methods of blowing up old buildings for commercial purposes over the next five years. Method One (implosion) is relatively low in risk for this business and will carry a 12 percent discount rate. Method Two (explosion) is less expensive to perform but more dangerous and will call for a higher discount rate of 16 percent. Either method will require an initial capital outlay of $75,000. The inflows from projected business over the next five years are given below. Which method should be selected using net present value analysis? (BH, p. 399, #8)

Year	Method 1	Method 2
====	========	========
1	$ 18,000	$ 20,000
2	$ 24,000	$ 25,000
3	$ 34,000	$ 35,000
4	$ 26,000	$ 28,000
5	$ 14,000	$ 15,000

46. Consider the following projects. Calculate the profitability index for Projects A and B assuming a 20 percent cost of capital. Use the profitability index rule to determine which project(s) you should accept if (i) you could undertake both and (ii) if you could undertake only one. (BMM, p. 177, #26)

Year	Project A	Project B
0	- $ 2,100	- $ 2,100
1	$ 2,000	$ 1,440
2	$ 1,200	$ 1,728

47. The management of Spartan Stamping Corporation is debating the purchase of a new reflex arm assembly to improve worker safety on one of its production lines. Two assemblies are currently under consideration with different expected future costs. If cost is the primary consideration, which of these mutually-exclusive alternatives should the company select? Assume a 15 percent hurdle rate for both alternatives.

	Assembly A	Assembly B
Initial Outlay	- $60,000	- $75,000
Useful Life	6 years	5 years
Annual Operating Costs		
Year 1	- $10,000	- $ 5,000
Year 2	- $11,000	- $ 6,000
Year 3	- $12,000	- $ 7,000
Year 4	- $13,000	- $ 8,000
Year 5	- $14,000	- $ 9,000
Year 6	- $15,000	

48. The Army Corps of Engineers is considering two alternatives to reduce future damages due to flooding on the Potomac River near Harpers Ferry, West Virginia. The problem is most acute where the river bends sharply forming a "buttonhook." One proposal is to channel through the bend in the river, leaving an island of limited commercial value. An alternative solution is to construct a dam and reservoir, which will result in a large section of unusable farmland. The values of these associated losses are estimated at -$25,000 and -$60,000 per year, respectively.

If no action is taken, damages are projected to continue at a rate of $3.5 million per year. The channel proposal would reduce this figure to $750,000 per year, while the dam and reservoir plan would entail losses of only $300,000 per year.

Determine the net present value and equivalent annual annuity for each proposal using the additional data given below. Assume a hurdle rate of 10 percent. Which project do you recommend?

	Channel	Dam/Reservoir
Initial Cost	- $12.5 million	- $17.3 million
Operating Costs	- $ 275,000/yr	- $ 350,000/yr
Useful Life	10 years	14 years

49. Phoenix Industries has pulled off a miraculous recovery. Four years ago it was near bankruptcy. Today, it announced a $1 per share dividend to be paid a year from now, the first dividend since the crisis. Analysts expect dividends to increase by $1 a year for another 2 years. After the third year (in which dividends are $3 per share), dividend growth is expected to settle down to a more moderate long-term growth rate of 6 percent. If the firm's investors expect to earn a return of 14 percent on this stock, what must be its price? (BMM, p. 141, #40)

50. The present value of the stream of cash flows shown below is $15,000 at a discount rate of 10 percent. What is the *approximate* value of the cash flow labeled "X"? Note that the $500 cash flows beginning in Year 5 continue *ad infinitum*.

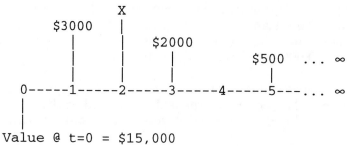

```
                    X
     $3000          |
        |           |     $2000
        |           |        |
        |           |        |         $500  ...  ∞
        |           |        |            |
    0-----1-----2-----3-----4-----5---...  ∞
    |
    |
   Value @ t=0 = $15,000
```

51. The Yurdone Corporation wants to set up a private cemetery business. According to the CFO, Barry M. Deep, business is "looking up." As a result, the cemetery project will provide a net cash inflow of $25,000 for the firm during the first year, and the cash flows are projected to grow at a rate of 7 percent per year forever. The project requires an initial investment of $300,000. If Yurdone requires a 16 percent return on investment, should the cemetery business be started? The company is somewhat unsure about the assumption of a 7 percent growth rate in its cash flows. At what constant growth rate would the company just break even if it still required a 16 percent return on investment? (RWJ Fundamentals, p. 277, #23)

52. A noted Swiss knife manufacturer prides itself on the quality of its products. A representative sample of knives destined for the United States was recently examined as part of the firm's quality control program. What is the mean and standard deviation of defective knives per 200-knife shipping carton?

Shipment	Defects	Shipment	Defects
========	=======	========	=======
1	1	7	1
2	0	8	0
3	0	9	2
4	1	10	1
5	2	11	3
6	1		

53. The distribution of exam scores for Mr. Overstreet's COM 371 class is shown below. Compute the mean and standard deviation on this exam.

95	77
90	63
75	75
82	85
84	73
86	99
88	80
55	92

54. Based on the following information, calculate the expected return. (RWJ Essentials, p. 315, #6)

State of Economy	Probability of State of Economy	Rate of Return if State Occurs
Recession	0.10	-0.09
Normal	0.70	0.11
Boom	0.20	0.28

55. You own a portfolio that is 60 percent invested in Stock X, 25 percent in Stock Y, and 15 percent in Stock Z. the expected returns on these three stocks are 10 percent, 17 percent, and 28 percent, respectively. What is the expected return on the portfolio?

56. Reactive Industries has the following capital structure. Its corporate tax rate is 35 percent. What is its weighted average cost of capital (WACC)? (BMM, p. 314, #8)

Security	Market Value	Required Rate of Return
Debt	$20 million	8 %
Preferred stock	$10 million	10 %
Common stock	$50 million	15 %

57. Larry's Athletic Lounge is planning an expansion program to increase the sophistication of its exercise equipment. Larry is considering some new equipment priced at $20,000 with an estimated life of five years. Larry is not sure how many members the new equipment will attract, but he estimates his increased yearly cash flows for each of the next five years will have the following probability distribution. Larry's cost of capital is 14 percent. What is the expected value of the cash flow? The value you compute will apply to each of the 5 years. What is the expected net present value? Should Larry buy the new equipment? (BH, p. 400, #9)

Probability	Cash Flow
===========	=========
.2	$2,400
.3	4,800
.4	6,000
.1	7,200

58. Platypus Products' historical sales figures for the past seven years are shown below. Use linear regression to forecast 1998 expected sales.

1991	$ 40,000
1992	$ 43,000
1993	$ 47,000
1994	$ 45,000
1995	$ 50,000
1996	$ 55,000
1997	$ 65,000

59. What is the beta coefficient of Whiz-Bang Corporation, given the historical return series shown below?

S&P 500	Whiz-Bang
=======	=========
-7.13	-8.21
0.85	1.64
2.40	1.61
-2.73	-0.58
8.80	6.37
-0.89	1.29
-0.52	-0.61
-9.91	-6.98
-5.25	-0.07
-0.67	3.87
5.82	4.06
2.45	2.04

60. According to a Cree Indian proverb, "Only after the last tree has been cut down, only after the last river has been poisoned, only after the last fish has been caught, only then will mankind discover that money cannot be eaten." World fishery stocks have declined in recent years, in some cases precipitously. The data shown below is for bay scallops. If the annual U.S. bay scallop catch follows a linear trend, when will the last bay scallop be caught?

Year	Catch (000s lb)
1983	2,338
1984	1,728
1985	1,331
1986	735
1987	580
1988	569
1989	274
1990	539
1991	438
1992	356

ANSWERS

1.

HP-10B	EL-733A	BA II Plus
-1.00 `PV`	-1.00 `PV`	-1.00 `PV`
6.00 `N`	6.00 `n`	6.00 `N`
4.00 `I/YR`	4.00 `i`	4.00 `I/Y`
`FV` 1.2653	`COMP` `FV` 1.2653	`CPT` `FV` 1.2653

$FVIF_{(4\%, 6)} = 1.2653$

HP-10B	EL-733A	BA II Plus
-1.00 `PMT`	-1.00 `PMT`	-1.00 `PMT`
30.00 `N`	30.00 `n`	30.00 `N`
6.50 `I/YR`	6.50 `i`	6.50 `I/Y`
`PV` 13.0587	`COMP` `PV` 13.0587	`CPT` `PV` 13.0587

$PVAF_{(6.5\%, 30)} = 13.0587$

2.

HP-10B	EL-733A	BA II Plus
-2,000 `PV`	-2'000 `PV`	-2,000 `PV`
173 `N`	173 `n`	173 `N`
5 `I/YR`	5 `i`	5 `I/Y`
`FV` 9,263,577	`COMP` `FV` 9'263'577	`CPT` `FV` 9,263,577

$FV = \$2,000 \cdot FVIF_{(5\%, 173)} = \$9,263,577.41$

3.

HP-10B	EL-733A	BA II Plus
-425.00 `FV`	-425.00 `FV`	-425.00 `FV`
23.00 `N`	23.00 `n`	23.00 `N`
7.50 `I/YR`	7.50 `i`	7.50 `I/Y`
`PV` 80.54	`COMP` `PV` 80.54	`CPT` `PV` 80.54

$PV = \$425 \text{ million} \cdot PVIF_{(7.50\%, 23)} = \$80.54 \text{ million}$

4.

HP-10B	EL-733A	BA II Plus
-1,000.00 [PMT]	-1'000.00 [PMT]	-1,000.00 [PMT]
15.00 [N]	15.00 [n]	15.00 [N]
8.50 [I/YR]	8.50 [i]	8.50 [I/Y]
[FV] 28,232.27	[COMP] [FV] 28'232.27	[CPT] [FV] 28,232.27

$$FV = \$1,000 \cdot FVAF_{(8.50\%,\ 15)} = \$28,232.27$$

If one were to make annual deposits of \$1,000 for the next 45 years, the balance would be \$450,530.40.

HP-10B	EL-733A	BA II Plus
-1,000.00 [PMT]	-1'000.00 [PMT]	-1,000.00 [PMT]
45.00 [N]	45.00 [n]	45.00 [N]
8.50 [I/YR]	8.50 [i]	8.50 [I/Y]
[FV] 450,530	[COMP] [FV] 450'530	[CPT] [FV] 450,530

$$FV = \$1,000 \cdot FVAF_{(8.50\%,\ 45)} = \$450,530.40$$

5.

HP-10B	EL-733A	BA II Plus
-2.99 [PV]	-2.99 [PV]	-2.99 [PV]
39.00 [N]	39.00 [n]	39.00 [N]
8,300.00 [FV]	8'300.00 [FV]	8,300.00 [FV]
[I/YR] 22.54	[COMP] [i] 22.54	[CPT] [I/Y] 22.54

$$\$8,300 = \$2.99 \cdot FVIF_{(x\%,\ 39)} \quad x = 22.54 \text{ percent}$$

6.

HP-10B	EL-733A	BA II Plus
3,000.00 [PMT]	3'000.00 [PMT]	3,000.00 [PMT]
5.00 [N]	5.00 [n]	5.00 [N]
12.00 [I/YR]	12.00 [i]	12.00 [I/Y]
[PV] -10,814	[COMP] [PV] -10'814	[CPT] [PV] -10,814

$PV = \$\ 3 \text{ million} \cdot PVAF_{(12.00\%,\ 5)} = \$\ 10.814 \text{ million}$

HP-10B	EL-733A	BA II Plus
2,000.00 [PMT]	2'000.00 [PMT]	2,000.00 [PMT]
5.00 [N]	5.00 [n]	5.00 [N]
12.00 [I/YR]	12.00 [i]	12.00 [I/Y]
[PV] -7,209	[COMP] [PV] -7'209	[CPT] [PV] -7,209

$PV = \$\ 2 \text{ million} \cdot PVAF_{(12.00\%,\ 5)} = \$\ 7.209 \text{ million}$

$ 7.209 million + $ 4 million = $ 11.209 million ... the receiver is better paid

7.

HP-10B	EL-733A	BA II Plus
-550,000 [PV]	-550'000 [PV]	-550,000 [PV]
5,000 [PMT]	5'000 [PMT]	5,000 [PMT]
0.75 [I/YR]	0.75 [i]	0.75 [I/Y]
[N] 233.26	[COMP] [n] 233.26	[CPT] [N] 233.26

Tom is indifferent between the two plans at a remaining life expectancy of 233 months (19 years, 5 months). After the age of 74 years and 5 months, the monthly payment plan is the preferred alternative.

8.

HP-10B	EL-733A	BA II Plus
500,000 [PMT]	500'000 [PMT]	500,000 [PMT]
40.00 [N]	40.00 [n]	40.00 [N]
12.00 [I/YR]	12.00 [i]	12.00 [I/Y]
[PV] -4,121,888	[COMP] [PV] -4'121,888	[CPT] [PV] -4,121,888

$PV = \$\ 500,000 \cdot PVAF_{(12.00\%,\ 40)} = \$4,121,888$

9.

HP-10B	EL-733A	BA II Plus
-25,000.00 [PV]	-25'000.00 [PV]	-25,000.00 [PV]
10.00 [N]	10.00 [n]	10.00 [N]
12.00 [I/YR]	12.00 [i]	12.00 [I/Y]
[FV] 77,646.21	[COMP] [FV] 77'646.21	[CPT] [FV] 77,646.21

$$FV = \$ 25,000 \cdot FVIF_{(12\%,\, 10)} = \$ 77,646.21$$

The card's projected value in ten years is $77,646.21.

10.

HP-10B	EL-733A	BA II Plus
-1,400.00 [PV]	-1'400.00 [PV]	-1,400.00 [PV]
3.00 [N]	3.00 [n]	3.00 [N]
2,100 [FV]	2'100 [FV]	2,100 [FV]
[I/YR] 14.47	[COMP] [i] 14.47	[CPT] [I/Y] 14.47

$$\$ 1,400 \cdot PVIF_{(x\%,\, 3)} = \$ 2,100$$

Mike earned a 14.47 percent annual rate of return on his investment.

11.

HP-10B	EL-733A	BA II Plus
-1,845.00 [PV]	-1'845.00 [PV]	-1,845.00 [PV]
36.00 [N]	36.00 [n]	36.00 [N]
56.00 [PMT]	56.00 [PMT]	56.00 [PMT]
[I/YR] 0.4872	[COMP] [i] 0.4872	[CPT] [I/Y] 0.4872

$$PV = \$2,050 - .10(\$2,050) = \$1,845 \qquad \$1,845 = \$56 \cdot PVAF_{(x\%,\, 36)}$$

x = 0.4872% per period

Without compounding: 0.4872 x 12 = 5.85 percent per year

With compounding: $(1.004872)^{12} - 1 = 0.0601 ==> 6.01$ percent per year

12.

HP-10B	EL-733A	BA II Plus
		2nd {BGN}
		2nd {SET}
		2nd {QUIT}
☐ {BEG/END}	BGN	
-42,000.00 PV	-42'000.00 PV	-42,000.00 PV
48.00 N	48.00 n	48.00 N
0.875 I/YR	0.875 i	0.875 I/Y
PMT 1,066.01	COMP PMT 1'066.01	CPT PMT 1,066.01

10.50% ÷ 12 months/year = 0.875% per period

The monthly lease payments will be $1,066.01.

13.

HP-10B	EL-733A	BA II Plus
-4,166.67 PMT	-4'166.67 PMT	-4,166.67 PMT
24.00 N	24.00 n	24.00 N
1.00 I/YR	1.00 i	1.00 I/Y
PV 88,514.18	COMP PV 88'514.18	CPT PV 88,514.18

$50,000 ÷ 12 months/year = $4,166.67 per period

2 years x 12 months/year = 24 periods

12.00% ÷ 12 months/year = 1.00% per period

$PV = \$ 4,166.67 \cdot PVAF_{(1.00\%, 24)} = \$ 88,514.18$

HP-10B	EL-733A	BA II Plus
-2,916.67 PMT	-2'916.67 PMT	-2,916.67 PMT
24.00 N	24.00 n	24.00 N
1.00 I/YR	1.00 i	1.00 I/Y
PV 61,959.95	COMP PV 61'959.95	CPT PV 61,959.95

$35,000 ÷ 12 months/year = $ 2,916.67 per period

$PV = \$ 2,916.67 \cdot PVAF_{(1.00\%, 24)} = \$ 61,959.95 + \$30,000 = \$ 91,959.95$ At this interest rate, the second arrangement is preferable to the first.

14.

HP-10B	EL-733A	BA II Plus
4.00 ☐ {P/YR}	4.00 [2ndF] {→EFF}	[2nd] {IConv}
7.50 ☐ {NOM%}	7.50	7.50 [ENTER]
☐ {EFF%} 7.71	[COMP] [=] 7.71	[↓] [↓]
		4.00 [ENTER]
		[↑] [CPT] 7.71

HP-10B	EL-733A	BA II Plus
2.00 ☐ {P/YR}	2.00 [2ndF] {→EFF}	[2nd] {IConv}
10.00 ☐ {NOM%}	10.00	10.00 [ENTER]
☐ {EFF%} 10.25	[COMP] [=] 10.25	[↓] [↓]
		2.00 [ENTER]
		[↑] [CPT] 10.25

You should borrow from Last National Bank, as it charges the lowest **effective** annual rate of interest.

15. Financial calculators offer no special advantage in solving this problem. However, the large numbers involved (23% per *month*!) often leads students to distrust their answers. If inflation were only 1 percent per month, the annual rate would equal $(1.01)^{12} - 1 = .1268 \Longrightarrow 12.68$ percent. A monthly inflation rate of 23% yields an annual rate of $(1.23)^{12} - 1 = 10.99 \Longrightarrow 1,099$ percent!

16.

HP-10B	EL-733A	BA II Plus
-8,000.00 [PV]	-8'000.00 [PV]	-8,000.00 [PV]
48.00 [N]	48.00 [n]	48.00 [N]
0.833 [I/YR]	0.833 [i]	0.833 [I/Y]
[PMT] 202.88	[COMP] [PMT] 202.88	[CPT] [PMT] 202.88

10.00% ÷ 12 months/year = 0.833% per period

$8,000 = PMT \cdot PVAF_{(0.833\%, \, 48)}$ PMT = $202.88

(answer continued on next page)

HP-10B		EL-733A		BA II Plus	
12.00 □ {P/YR}		12.00 2ndF {→EFF}		2nd {IConv}	
10.00 □ {NOM%}		10.00		10.00 ENTER	
□ {EFF%} 10.47		COMP = 10.47		↓ ↓	
				12.00 ENTER	
				↑ CPT 10.47	

The loan has an effective annual interest rate of 10.47 percent.

17.

HP-10B		EL-733A		BA II Plus	
-10,000.00 PV		-10'000.00 PV		-10,000.00 PV	
0.9917 I/YR		0.9917 i		0.9917 I/Y	
200.00 PMT		200.00 PMT		200.00 PMT	
N 69.40		COMP n 69.40		CPT N 69.40	

11.90% ÷ 12 months/year = 0.9917% per period

$10,000 = $200 · PVAF$_{(0.9917\%, N)}$ N = 69.40 months

HP-10B		EL-733A		BA II Plus	
-10,000.00 PV		-10'000.00 PV		-10,000.00 PV	
0.4917 I/YR		0.4917 i		0.4917 I/Y	
200.00 PMT		200.00 PMT		200.00 PMT	
N 57.53		COMP n 57.53		CPT N 57.53	

5.90% ÷ 12 months/year = 0.4917% per period

$10,000 = $200 · PVAF$_{(0.4917\%, N)}$ N = 57.53 months

If there is no fee, transferring your balance to the 5.9% card will allow you to pay it off about 12 months earlier than if it were left on the 11.9% card. A 2% transfer fee increases the present value on the 5.9% card to $10,200 and slightly lengthens the payoff period to 58.86 months.

18.

HP-10B	EL-733A	BA II Plus
4.00 ☐ {P/YR}	4.00 [2ndF] {→APR}	[2nd] {IConv}
12.00 ☐ {EFF%}	12.00	[↓]
☐ {NOM%} 11.49	[COMP] [=] 11.49	12.00 [ENTER]
		[↓]
		4.00 [ENTER]
		[↑] [↑] [CPT] 11.49

A nominal rate of 11.49 percent, compounded quarterly is equivalent to a 12 percent effective rate.

19.

HP-10B	EL-733A	BA II Plus
-50,000 [PV]	-50'000 [PV]	-50,000 [PV]
5 [N]	5 [n]	5 [N]
12 [I/YR]	12 [i]	12 [I/Y]
[FV] 88,117	[COMP] [FV] 88'117	[CPT] [FV] 88,117

$$FV = \$\,50{,}000 \cdot FVIF_{(12\%,\,5)} = \$\,88{,}117$$

HP-10B	EL-733A	BA II Plus
-88,117 [PV]	-88'117 [PV]	-88,117 [PV]
10 [N]	10 [n]	10 [N]
12 [I/YR]	12 [i]	12 [I/Y]
[PMT] 15,595	[COMP] [PMT] 15'595	[CPT] [PMT] 15,595

$$\$88{,}117 = PMT \cdot PVAF_{(12\%,\,10)} \qquad PMT = \$15{,}595$$

20. A cash flow diagram is practically essential to solving this problem. First determine the future value of his investments at t=55. Then set this number equal to the present value of an *annuity due* for his remaining withdrawals.

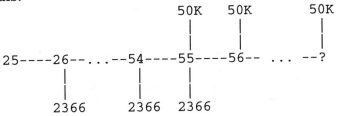

HP-10B		EL-733A		BA II Plus	
-2,366	PMT	-2'366	PMT	-2,366	PMT
30	N	30	n	30	N
10	I/YR	10	i	10	I/Y
FV	389,193	COMP FV	389'193	CPT FV	389,193

HP-10B		EL-733A		BA II Plus	
				2nd {BGN}	
				2nd {SET}	
☐ {BEG/END}		BGN		2nd {QUIT}	
389,193	PV	389'193	PV	389,193	PV
-50,000	PMT	-50'000	PMT	-50,000	PMT
10	I/YR	10	i	10	I/Y
N	12.90	COMP n	12.90	CPT N	12.90

Odysseus will be 55 + 12.9 ≈ 68 years old when he makes his last withdrawal.

21.

HP-10B	EL-733A	BA II Plus
100,000 [FV]	100'000 [FV]	100,000 [FV]
20 [N]	20 [n]	20 [N]
4 [I/YR]	4 [i]	4 [I/Y]
[PMT] -3,358	[COMP] [PMT] -3'358	[CPT] [PMT] -3,358

With no change in interest rates, semiannual payments of $3,358 should allow you to meet your goal of $100,000 in ten years. The value of your deposits at t=4 is $ 3,358 \cdot \text{FVAF}_{(4\%,\ 4)} = \$ 14,259$.

Compounded forward for the remaining 16 periods at 5% per period, $ 14,259 \cdot \text{FVIF}_{(5\%,\ 16)} = \$31,125$. Subtracting $31,125 from $100,000 gives a new goal of $68,874.

HP-10B	EL-733A	BA II Plus
68,874 [FV]	68,874 [FV]	68,874 [FV]
16 [N]	16 [n]	16 [N]
5 [I/YR]	5 [i]	5 [I/Y]
[PMT] -2,911	[COMP] [PMT] -2'911	[CPT] [PMT] -2,911

Under these assumptions, the revised payments should be approximately $2,911 per semiannual period.

22. This problem is best done in parts. First, draw the cash flow diagram.
NOTE: "Today" is at t=5.

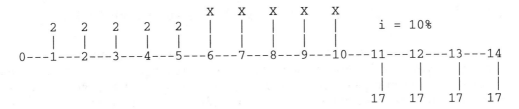

Then determine the value of your sister's college expenses in Year 10, i.e.,
$17,000 \cdot \text{PVAF}_{(10\%,\, 4)} = \$\,53,887$.

HP-10B		EL-733A		BA II Plus	
-17,000	PMT	-17'000	PMT	-17,000	PMT
4	N	4	n	4	N
10	I/YR	10	i	10	I/Y
PV	53,887	COMP PV	53'887	CPT PV	53,887

If your parents were to continue saving \$2,000 per year through Year 10, the
future value of their accumulation would be $\$2,000 \cdot \text{FVAF}_{(10\%,\, 10)} = \$\,31,875$.

HP-10B		EL-733A		BA II Plus	
-2,000	PMT	-2'000	PMT	-2,000	PMT
10	N	10	n	10	N
10	I/YR	10	i	10	I/Y
FV	31,875	COMP FV	31'875	CPT FV	31,875

The shortfall between planned expenses and planned savings equals $53,887 −
$31,875 = $22,012. To remedy this, your parents should plan on saving an
additional $3,606 per year for a total payment of $5,606.

HP-10B		EL-733A		BA II Plus	
22,012	FV	22'012	PMT	22,012	PMT
5	N	5	n	5	N
10	I/YR	10	i	10	I/Y
PMT	3,606	COMP FV	-3'606	CPT FV	-3,606

$\text{PMT} \cdot \text{FVAF}_{(10\%,\, 5)} = \$\,22,012.$ $\text{PMT} = \$3,606.$

23. Daily interest rate = 5 percent ÷ 365 = 0.000137 $\dfrac{\$0.50}{0.000137} = \$3,650$

24. $\dfrac{\$6.30}{0.09} = \$70$ Ultra Corporation's preferred stock should sell for $70.

25. This problem requires some data manipulation before it can be solved as a "standard" perpetuity. First, because the cash flows occur every *other* year, we must define our periods as two-year intervals. Second, we will need to compute the effective interest rate for this two-year period. And third, because the first cash flow occurs one year from now (really one-half period from now), we'll solve for the present value of the perpetuity one-half period earlier, and then compound this value forward one-half period.

The effective *biannual* interest rate = $\left(1 + \dfrac{0.16}{365}\right)^{730} - 1 = .3770 \Rightarrow 37.70$ percent

The corresponding cash flow diagram for this process is:

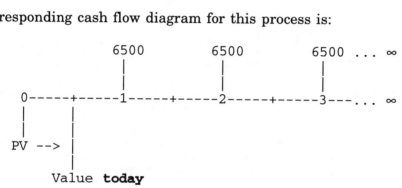

The value of this investment *one-half period earlier* is $\dfrac{\$6,500}{0.3770} = \$17,241.38$

Compounding this value forward at an effective rate of 37.70 for one-half period gives us the value of this investment **today**.

HP-10B	EL-733A	BA II Plus
-17,241.38 [PV]	-17'241.38 [PV]	-17,241.38 [PV]
0.50 [N]	0.50 [n]	0.50 [N]
37.70 [I/YR]	37.70 [i]	37.70 [I/Y]
[FV] 20,232.01	[COMP] [FV] 20,232.01	[CPT] [FV] 20,232.01

FV = $ 17,241.38 · FVIF$_{(37.70\%,\ 0.5)}$ = $ 20,232.01

(answer continued on next page)

The value of the infinite cash flow stream remains $17,241.38, regardless of when it begins. If the first payment does not occur until four years (two periods, t=2) from now, this will be the value at t=1. "Double discounting" this figure back to t=0 yields a value of $12,520.97 **today**.

HP-10B		EL-733A		BA II Plus	
-17,241.38	FV	-17'241.38	PV	-17,241.38	PV
1.00	N	1.00	n	1.00	N
37.70	I/YR	37.70	i	37.70	I/Y
PV	12,520.97	COMP FV	12'520.97	CPT FV	12,520.97

26. Price of common stock = $\dfrac{\$2.00}{.12-.06}$ = $33.33

27. Return on common stock = $\dfrac{\$4.90}{\$70}$ + .06 = 13.00 percent

28.

HP-10B		EL-733A		BA II Plus	
80.00	PMT	80.00	PMT	80.00	PMT
1,000.00	FV	1'000.00	FV	1,000.00	FV
9.00	N	9.00	n	9.00	N
9.00	I/YR	9.00	i	9.00	I/Y
PV	-940.05	COMP PV	-940.05	CPT PV	-940.05

Bondholders receive (.08)($ 1,000) = $80 in interest payments each year. The bond's price should be $940.05. If the yield to maturity falls to 7 percent, the bond's price will increase to $1,065.15 (above its par value). Bonds sell above par when the yield to maturity is less than the coupon rate.

29.

HP-10B		EL-733A		BA II Plus	
40.00	PMT	40.00	PMT	40.00	PMT
1,000.00	FV	1'000.00	FV	1,000.00	FV
50.00	N	50.00	n	50.00	N
5.00	I/YR	5.00	i	5.00	I/Y
PV	-817.44	COMP PV	-817.44	CPT PV	-817.44

Price = $817.44

30.

HP-10B		EL-733A		BA II Plus	
-825.00	PV	-825.00	PV	-825.00	PV
13.00	N	13.00	n	13.00	N
7.00	I/YR	7.00	i	7.00	I/Y
1,000.00	FV	1'000.00	FV	1,000.00	FV
PMT	49.06	COMP PMT	49.06	CPT PMT	49.06

Merton Enterprises' bonds should carry an annual coupon rate of 4.906 percent of par. 0.04906 x $1,000 = $49.06

31.

HP-10B		EL-733A		BA II Plus	
-921.69	PV	-921.69	PV	-921.69	PV
45.00	PMT	45.00	PMT	45.00	PMT
1,000.00	FV	1'000.00	FV	1,000.00	FV
30.00	N	30.00	n	30.00	N
I/YR	5.01	COMP i	5.01	CPT I/Y	5.01

The semiannual yield on the company's existing bonds is 5.01 percent. As BDJ wants its new bonds to sell at par, it should set the coupon rate at 2 x 5.01 = 10.02 percent.

32.

HP-10B	EL-733A	BA II Plus
-1,050.00 [PV]	-1'050.00 [PV]	-1,050.00 [PV]
40.00 [PMT]	40.00 [PMT]	40.00 [PMT]
1,000.00 [FV]	1'000.00 [FV]	1,000.00 [FV]
18.00 [N]	18.00 [n]	18.00 [N]
[I/YR] 3.62	[COMP] [i] 3.62	[CPT] [I/Y] 3.62

The new yield to maturity = 2 x 3.84 = 7.23 percent.

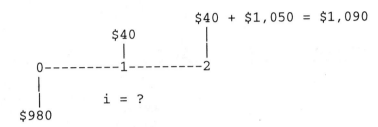

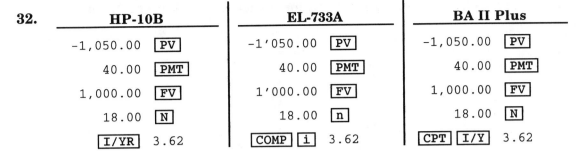

HP-10B	EL-733A	BA II Plus
-980.00 [PV]	-980.00 [PV]	-980.00 [PV]
40.00 [PMT]	40.00 [PMT]	40.00 [PMT]
1,050.00 [FV]	1'050.00 [FV]	1,050.00 [FV]
2.00 [N]	2.00 [n]	2.00 [N]
[I/YR] 7.52	[COMP] [i] 7.52	[CPT] [I/Y] 7.52

Your annualized rate of return for this one-year holding period was
2 x 7.52 = 15.04 percent.

33. The schedule of coupon payments for Bonds M and N are as follows:

Time	Bond M	Bond N	
====	=======	======	
0	$ 0	$ 0	
1	0	0	
...	0	0	
12	0	0	
13	1,000	0	
...	1,000	0	
28	1,000	0	
25	1,750	0	
...	1,750	0	
39	1,750	0	* $1,750 coupon payment
40	21,750*	20,000	+ $20,000 repayment of principal

HP-10B	**EL-733A**	**BA II Plus**
0 [CFj]	0 [CFi]	[CF]
0 [CFj]	0 [CFi]	[2nd] {CLR Work}
12 [ ] {Nj}	12 [CFi]	0 [ENTER] [↓]
1,000 [CFj]	1'000 [2ndF] {Ni}	0 [ENTER] [↓]
16 [ ] {Nj}	16 [CFi]	12 [ENTER] [↓]
1,750 [CFj]	1'750 [CFi]	1,000 [ENTER] [↓]
11 [ ] {Nj}	11 [2ndF] {Ni}	16 [ENTER] [↓]
21,750 [CFj]	21'750 [CFi]	1,750 [ENTER] [↓]
7 [I/YR]	7 [i]	11 [ENTER] [↓]
[ ] {NPV} 7,620.58	[NPV] 7'620.58	21,750 [ENTER] [↓]
		1 [ENTER] [↓]
		[NPV]
		7 [ENTER]
		[↓] [CPT] 7,620.58

Bond M has a current price of $7,620.58, while Bond N's price is $1,335.61.

HP-10B	**EL-733A**	**BA II Plus**
20,000 [FV]	20'000 [FV]	20,000 [FV]
40 [N]	40 [n]	40 [N]
7 [I/YR]	7 [i]	7 [I/Y]
[PV] −1,335.61	[COMP] [PV] −1'335.61	[CPT] [PV] −1,335.61

34.   **Hewlett Packard HP-10B**

-5,000.00	[PV]		
2.00	[I/YR]		
20	[N]		
	[PMT]	305.78	<== Payment amount

Principal portion of 3rd payment

3	[INPUT]	[ ]	{AMORT}	[=]	91.69	<== Interest
				[=]	214.10	<== Principal
				[=]	-4,370.22	<== Balance @ t=3

Interest from t=1 to t=4

1	[INPUT]	4	[ ]	{AMORT}	[=]	374.98	<== Total interest
					[=]	848.16	<== Total principal
					[=]	-4,151.84	<== Balance

Sharp Electronics EL-733A

-5'000.00	[PV]			
2.00	[i]			
20.00	[n]			
	[COMP]	[PMT]	305.78	<== Payment amount

Principal portion of 3rd payment

3	[AMRT]	214.10	<== Principal
	[AMRT]	91.69	<== Interest
	[AMRT]	-4'370.22	<== Balance @ t=3

Interest from t=1 to t=4

1	[P₁/P₂]	4	[P₁/P₂] [ACC]	848.16	<== Total principal
			[ACC]	374.98	<== Total interest

```
  -5,000.00  [PV]
       2.00  [I/Y]
      20.00  [N]
[CPT] [PMT]    305.78   <== Payment amount
```

[2nd] {Amort} [2nd] {CLR Work}

Principal portion of 3rd payment

```
         3 [ENTER] [↓]
         3 [ENTER] [↓]   4,370.22  <== Balance @ t=3
                  [↓]     -214.10  <== Principal
                  [↓]      -91.69  <== Interest
```

Interest from t=1 to t=4

[2nd] {CLR Work}

```
         1 [ENTER] [↓]
         4 [ENTER] [↓]   4,151.84  <== Balance @ t=4
                  [↓]     -848.16  <== Total principal
                  [↓]     -374.98  <== Total interest
```

35. _____**Hewlett Packard HP-10B**_____

$$-100,000.00 \boxed{\text{PV}}$$

$$804.62 \boxed{\text{PMT}}$$

$$360.00 \boxed{\text{N}}$$

$$\boxed{\text{I/YR}} \quad 0.75 \quad <== \text{ interest rate/period}$$

$$= 9.00\% \text{ per year}$$

Remaining balance at t=120

120 $\boxed{\text{INPUT}}$ $\boxed{}$ {AMORT} $\boxed{=}$ 671.72 <== Interest

$\boxed{=}$ 132.90 <== Principal

$\boxed{=}$ -89,429.69 <== Balance @ t=120

Remaining balance at t=240

240 $\boxed{\text{INPUT}}$ $\boxed{}$ {AMORT} $\boxed{=}$ 478.83 <== Interest

$\boxed{=}$ 325.79 <== Principal

$\boxed{=}$ -63,518.17 <== Balance @ t=240

_____**Sharp Electronics EL-733A**_____

$$-100'000.00 \boxed{\text{PV}}$$

$$804.62 \boxed{\text{PMT}}$$

$$360.00 \boxed{\text{n}}$$

$$\boxed{\text{COMP}} \boxed{\text{i}} \quad 0.75 \quad <== \text{ interest rate/period}$$

$$= 9.00\% \text{ per year}$$

Remaining balance at t=120

120 $\boxed{\text{AMRT}}$ 132.90 <== Principal

$\boxed{\text{AMRT}}$ 671.72 <== Interest

$\boxed{\text{AMRT}}$ -89'429.69 <== Balance @ t=120

Remaining balance at t=240

240 $\boxed{\text{AMRT}}$ 325.79 <== Principal

$\boxed{\text{AMRT}}$ 478.83 <== Interest

$\boxed{\text{AMRT}}$ -63'518.17 <== Balance @ t=240

$$-100,000.00 \quad \boxed{\text{PV}}$$

$$804.62 \quad \boxed{\text{PMT}}$$

$$360.00 \quad \boxed{\text{N}}$$

$\boxed{\text{CPT}} \boxed{\text{I/Y}}$ 0.75   <== interest rate/period

= 9.00% per year

$\boxed{\text{2nd}}$ {Amort} $\boxed{\text{2nd}}$ {CLR Work}

Remaining balance at t=120

120 $\boxed{\text{ENTER}} \boxed{\downarrow}$

120 $\boxed{\text{ENTER}} \boxed{\downarrow}$ -89,429.69   <== Balance @ t=120

$\boxed{\downarrow}$ 132.90   <== Principal

$\boxed{\downarrow}$ 671.72   <== Interest

Remaining balance at t=240

$\boxed{\text{2nd}}$ {CLR Work}

240 $\boxed{\text{ENTER}} \boxed{\downarrow}$

240 $\boxed{\text{ENTER}} \boxed{\downarrow}$ -63,518.17   <== Balance @ t=240

$\boxed{\downarrow}$ 325.79   <== Principal

$\boxed{\downarrow}$ 478.83   <== Interest

36.

HP-10B		EL-733A		BA II Plus	
-100,000.00	[PV]	-100'000.00	[PV]	-100,000.00	[PV]
360.00	[N]	360.00	[n]	360.00	[N]
1.00	[I/YR]	1.00	[i]	1.00	[I/Y]
[PMT] 1,028.61		[COMP] [PMT] 1'028.61		[CPT] [PMT] 1,028.61	

The monthly payment is $1,028.61

HP-10B		EL-733A		BA II Plus	
-98,000.00	[PV]	-98'000.00	[PV]	-98,000.00	[PV]
360.00	[N]	360.00	[n]	360.00	[N]
1,028.61	[PMT]	1'028.61	[PMT]	1,028.61	[PMT]
[I/YR] 1.023		[COMP] [i] 1.023		[CPT] [I/Y] 1.023	

The effective annual interest rate on this loan is $(1.01023)^{12} - 1 = 31.4$ percent

37.

HP-10B		EL-733A		BA II Plus	
-200,000	[PV]	-200'000	[PV]	-200,000	[PV]
1,000	[PMT]	1'000	[PMT]	1,000	[PMT]
360	[N]	360	[n]	360	[N]
0.5417	[I/YR]	0.5417	[i]	0.5417	[I/Y]
[FV] 292,262		[COMP] [FV] 292'262		[CPT] [FV] 292,262	

6.50% ÷ 12 months/year ≈ 0.5417% per period

The "balloon" portion equals $292,262. Your final payment equals $292,262 + $1,000 = $293,262.

38.

HP-10B		EL-733A		BA II Plus		
0	CFj	0	CFi	CF		
2,900	CFj	2'900	CFi	2nd	{CLR Work}	
3,770	CFj	3'770	CFi	0	ENTER	↓
4,640	CFj	4'640	CFi	2,900	ENTER	↓
5,510	CFj	5'510	CFi	1	ENTER	↓
6,380	CFj	6'380	CFi	3,770	ENTER	↓
7,250	CFj	7'250	CFi	1	ENTER	↓
8,120	CFj	8'120	CFi	4,640	ENTER	↓
8,990	CFj	8'990	CFi	1	ENTER	↓
9,860	CFj	9'860	CFi	5,510	ENTER	↓
10,730	CFj	10'730	CFi	1	ENTER	↓
12	I/YR	12	i	6,380	ENTER	↓
☐ {NPV}	34,006.70	NPV	34'006.70	1	ENTER	↓
				7,250	ENTER	↓
				1	ENTER	↓
				8,120	ENTER	↓
				1	ENTER	↓
				8,990	ENTER	↓
				1	ENTER	↓
				9,860	ENTER	↓
				1	ENTER	↓
				10,730	ENTER	↓
				1	ENTER	↓
				NPV	ENTER	↓
				12	ENTER	
				↓ CPT	34,006.70	

The present value of "Big Dog" Robinson's contract with the Bucks is $34,006,704.09.

39. A cash flow diagram is helpful to illustrate this problem.

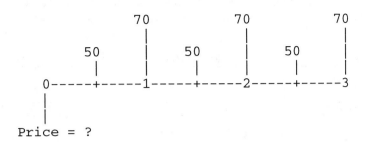

HP-10B	EL-733A	BA II Plus	
0.00 CFj	0.00 CFi	CF	
50.00 CFj	50.00 CFi	2nd {CLR Work}	
70.00 CFj	70.00 CFi	0.00 ENTER ↓	
50.00 CFj	50.00 CFi	50.00 ENTER ↓	
70.00 CFj	70.00 CFi	1.00 ENTER ↓	
50.00 CFj	50.00 CFi	70.00 ENTER ↓	
70.00 CFj	70.00 CFi	1.00 ENTER ↓	
4.00 I/YR	4.00 i	50.00 ENTER ↓	
☐ {NPV} 313.50	NPV 313.50	1.00 ENTER ↓	
		70.00 ENTER ↓	
		1.00 ENTER ↓	
		50.00 ENTER ↓	
		1.00 ENTER ↓	
		70.00 ENTER ↓	
		1.00 ENTER ↓	
		NPV	
		4.00 ENTER	
		↓ CPT 313.50	

The most one should pay for a three-year FizzBuzz is $313.50.

40. The fastest way to determine the future value of an uneven series of cash flows on an electronic calculator is to discount them all back to zero and then compound the result forward the required number of periods.

HP-10B		EL-733A		BA II Plus	
0.00	CFj	0.00	CFi	CF	
500.00	CFj	500.00	CFi	2nd	{CLR Work}
600.00	CFj	600.00	CFi	0.00	ENTER ↓
700.00	CFj	700.00	CFi	500.00	ENTER ↓
800.00	CFj	800.00	CFi	1	ENTER ↓
7.00	I/YR	7.00	i	600.00	ENTER ↓
□ {NPV} 2,173.08		NPV 2'173.08		1	ENTER ↓
				700.00	ENTER ↓
				1	ENTER ↓
				800.00	ENTER ↓
				1	ENTER ↓
				NPV	
				7.00	ENTER
				↓ CPT 2,173.08	

HP-10B		EL-733A		BA II Plus	
-2,173.08	PV	-2'173.08	PV	-2,173.08	PV
4.00	N	4.00	n	4.00	N
7.00	I/YR	7.00	i	7.00	I/Y
FV 2,848.46		COMP FV 2'848.46		CPT FV 2,848.46	

At a 7% discount rate, the FV of this cash flow series is $2,848.46.

At a 10% discount rate, the FV of this cash flow series is $2,961.50.

At a 22% discount rate, the FV of this cash flow series is $3,454.96.

41.

HP-10B		EL-733A		BA II Plus	
−243,715	$\boxed{\text{CFj}}$	−243′715	$\boxed{\text{CFi}}$		$\boxed{\text{CF}}$
75,429	$\boxed{\text{CFj}}$	75′429	$\boxed{\text{CFi}}$		$\boxed{\text{2nd}}$ {CLR Work}
153,408	$\boxed{\text{CFj}}$	153′408	$\boxed{\text{CFi}}$	−243,715	$\boxed{\text{ENTER}}$ $\boxed{\downarrow}$
102,389	$\boxed{\text{CFj}}$	102′389	$\boxed{\text{CFi}}$	75,429	$\boxed{\text{ENTER}}$ $\boxed{\downarrow}$
45,000	$\boxed{\text{CFj}}$	45′000	$\boxed{\text{CFi}}$	1	$\boxed{\text{ENTER}}$ $\boxed{\downarrow}$
0	$\boxed{\text{I/YR}}$	0	$\boxed{\text{i}}$	153,408	$\boxed{\text{ENTER}}$ $\boxed{\downarrow}$
$\boxed{}$ {NPV}	132,511	$\boxed{\text{NPV}}$ 132′511		1	$\boxed{\text{ENTER}}$ $\boxed{\downarrow}$
$\boxed{}${IRR/YR}	21.50	$\boxed{\text{IRR}}$ 21.50		102,389	$\boxed{\text{ENTER}}$ $\boxed{\downarrow}$
				1	$\boxed{\text{ENTER}}$ $\boxed{\downarrow}$
				45,000	$\boxed{\text{ENTER}}$ $\boxed{\downarrow}$
				1	$\boxed{\text{ENTER}}$ $\boxed{\downarrow}$
					$\boxed{\text{NPV}}$
				0	$\boxed{\text{ENTER}}$
				$\boxed{\downarrow}$ $\boxed{\text{CPT}}$	132,511
				$\boxed{\text{IRR}}$ $\boxed{\text{CPT}}$	21.50

Net present value = \$132,511 at a discount rate of zero. When the discount rate is infinite, NPV equals the initial outlay at t=0. When NPV = 0, the discount rate equals the internal rate of return (IRR).

42.

HP-10B	EL-733A	BA II Plus
-4.5 `CFj`	-4.5 `CFi`	`CF`
2.8 `CFj`	39 `2ndF` {Nᵢ}	`2nd` {CLR Work}
39 `☐` {Nⱼ}	2.8 `CFi`	-4.5 `ENTER` `↓`
-7.2 `CFj`	-7.2 `CFi`	2.8 `ENTER` `↓`
18 `I/YR`	18 `i`	39 `ENTER` `↓`
`☐` {NPV} 11.02	`NPV` 11.02	-7.2 `ENTER` `↓`
		1 `ENTER` `↓`
		`NPV`
		18 `ENTER`
		`↓` `CPT` 11.02

NPV of the proposed nuclear power plant = $11.02 million

Profitability Index = $(11.02 + 4.5) \div 4.5 = 3.45$

Equivalent Annual Annuity: $\$11.02 = X \cdot PVAF_{(18\%,\ 40)}$

HP-10B	EL-733A	BA II Plus
-11.02 `PV`	-11.02 `PV`	-11.02 `PV`
40.00 `N`	40.00 `n`	40.00 `N`
18.00 `I/YR`	18.00 `i`	18.00 `I/Y`
`PMT` 1.99	`COMP` `PMT` 1.99	`CPT` `PMT` 1.99

The equivalent annual annuity of the proposed nuclear plant = $1.99 million

43.

HP-10B		EL-733A		BA II Plus	
−110,000	[CFj]	−110'000	[CFi]	[CF]	
36,000	[CFj]	36'000	[CFi]	[2nd]	{CLR Work}
44,000	[CFj]	44'000	[CFi]	−110,000	[ENTER] [↓]
38,000	[CFj]	38'000	[CFi]	36,000	[ENTER] [↓]
−44,000	[CFj]	−44'000	[CFi]	1	[ENTER] [↓]
81,000	[CFj]	81'000	[CFi]	44,000	[ENTER] [↓]
11	[I/YR]	11	[i]	1	[ENTER] [↓]
[ ] {NPV}	5,014.49	[NPV]	5'014.49	38,000	[ENTER] [↓]
				1	[ENTER] [↓]
				−44,000	[ENTER] [↓]
				1	[ENTER] [↓]
				81,000	[ENTER] [↓]
				1	[ENTER] [↓]
				[NPV]	
				11	[ENTER]
				[↓] [CPT]	5,014.49

Because the project has a positive net present value of $5,014.49, it should be undertaken.

44. Project 1

HP-10B		EL-733A		BA II Plus	
-12,500	`CFj`	-12'500	`CFi`		`CF`
4,000	`CFj`	4'000	`CFi`		`2nd` {CLR Work}
5,000	`CFj`	5'000	`CFi`	-12,500	`ENTER` `↓`
6,000	`CFj`	6'000	`CFi`	4,000	`ENTER` `↓`
1,000	`CFj`	1'000	`CFi`	1	`ENTER` `↓`
`□` {IRR} 11.85		`IRR` 11.85		5,000	`ENTER` `↓`
11.00	`I/YR`	11.00	`i`	1	`ENTER` `↓`
`□` {NPV} 207.60		`NPV` 207.60		6,000	`ENTER` `↓`
				1	`ENTER` `↓`
				1,000	`ENTER` `↓`
				1	`ENTER` `↓`
				`IRR` `CPT` 11.85	
				`NPV`	
				11.00	`ENTER`
				`↓` `CPT` 207.60	

Project 2

HP-10B	EL-733A	BA II Plus
-12,500 `CFj`	-12'500 `CFi`	`CF`
1,000 `CFj`	1'000 `CFi`	`2nd` {CLR Work}
6,000 `CFj`	6'000 `CFi`	-12,500 `ENTER` `↓`
5,000 `CFj`	5'000 `CFi`	1,000 `ENTER` `↓`
4,000 `CFj`	4'000 `CFi`	1 `ENTER` `↓`
☐ {IRR} 9.53	`IRR` 9.53	6,000 `ENTER` `↓`
11.00 `I/YR`	11.00 `i`	1 `ENTER` `↓`
☐ {NPV} -438.48	`NPV` -438.48	5,000 `ENTER` `↓`
		1 `ENTER` `↓`
		4,000 `ENTER` `↓`
		1 `ENTER` `↓`
		`IRR` `CPT` 9.53
		`NPV`
		11.00 `ENTER`
		`↓` `CPT` -438.48

Project 1 has an IRR of 11.85% and an NPV (at 11%) of $207.60. Project 2 has an IRR of 9.53% and an NPV (at 11%) of -$438.48. The IRR decision rule is not appropriate for deciding which of two mutually-exclusive projects to accept. Because Project 1 has the higher NPV, it should be selected over Project 1. Indeed, because Project 2 has a negative NPV, it should *never* be selected.

45. Method 1

HP-10B	EL-733A	BA II Plus	
-75,000 [CFj]	-75'000 [CFi]	[CF]	
18,000 [CFj]	18'000 [CFi]	[2nd] {CLR Work}	
24,000 [CFj]	24'000 [CFi]	-75,000 [ENTER] [↓]	
34,000 [CFj]	34'000 [CFi]	18,000 [ENTER] [↓]	
26,000 [CFj]	26'000 [CFi]	1 [ENTER] [↓]	
14,000 [CFj]	14'000 [CFi]	24,000 [ENTER] [↓]	
12 [I/YR]	12 [i]	1 [ENTER] [↓]	
[ ] {NPV} 8,872.06	[NPV] 8'872.06	34,000 [ENTER] [↓]	
		1 [ENTER] [↓]	
		26,000 [ENTER] [↓]	
		1 [ENTER] [↓]	
		14,000 [ENTER] [↓]	
		1 [ENTER] [↓]	
		[NPV]	
		12 [ENTER]	
		[↓] [CPT] 8,872.06	

Method 2

HP-10B	EL-733A	BA II Plus
-75,000 CFj	-75'000 CFi	CF
20,000 CFj	20'000 CFi	2nd {CLR Work}
25,000 CFj	25'000 CFi	-75,000 ENTER ↓
35,000 CFj	35'000 CFi	20,000 ENTER ↓
28,000 CFj	28'000 CFi	1 ENTER ↓
15,000 CFj	15'000 CFi	25,000 ENTER ↓
16 I/YR	16 i	1 ENTER ↓
☐ {NPV} 5,849.32	NPV 5'849.32	35,000 ENTER ↓
		1 ENTER ↓
		28,000 ENTER ↓
		1 ENTER ↓
		15,000 ENTER ↓
		1 ENTER ↓
		NPV
		16 ENTER
		↓ CPT 5,849.32

Method 1 has the higher net present value and should be selected over Method 2.

46. **Project A**

HP-10B	EL-733A	BA II Plus
-2,100.00 [CFj]	-2'100.00 [CFi]	[CF]
2,000.00 [CFj]	2'000.00 [CFi]	[2nd] {CLR Work}
1,200.00 [CFj]	1'200.00 [CFi]	-2,100.00 [ENTER] [↓]
20.00 [I/YR]	20.00 [i]	2,000.00 [ENTER] [↓]
[□] {NPV} 400.00	[NPV] 400.00	1 [ENTER] [↓]
		1,200.00 [ENTER] [↓]
		1 [ENTER] [↓]
		[NPV]
		20.00 [ENTER]
		[↓] [CPT] 400.00

Project B

HP-10B	EL-733A	BA II Plus
-2,100.00 [CFj]	-2'100.00 [CFi]	[CF]
1,440.00 [CFj]	1'440.00 [CFi]	[2nd] {CLR Work}
1,728.00 [CFj]	1'728.00 [CFi]	-2,100.00 [ENTER] [↓]
20.00 [I/YR]	20.00 [i]	1,440.00 [ENTER] [↓]
[□] {NPV} 300.00	[NPV] 300.00	1 [ENTER] [↓]
		1,728.00 [ENTER] [↓]
		1 [ENTER] [↓]
		[NPV]
		20.00 [ENTER]
		[↓] [CPT] 300.00

Project A's profitability index = ($2,100 + 400) ÷ 2,100 =1.19. Project B's profitability index = ($2,100+ 300) ÷ 2,100 =1.14. As both projects have positive net present values, you should accept both, if possible. If you can undertake only one, Project A has the greater profitability index and delivers more "bang for the buck."

47. Because these projects have different lives, the equivalent annual annuity approach is the appropriate decision-making tool.

Assembly A

HP-10B	EL-733A	BA II Plus
-60,000 [CFj]	-60'000 [CFi]	[CF]
-10,000 [CFj]	-10'000 [CFi]	[2nd] {CLR Work}
-11,000 [CFj]	-11'000 [CFi]	-60,000 [ENTER] [↓]
-12,000 [CFj]	-12'000 [CFi]	-10,000 [ENTER] [↓]
-13,000 [CFj]	-13'000 [CFi]	1 [ENTER] [↓]
-14,000 [CFj]	-14'000 [CFi]	-11,000 [ENTER] [↓]
-15,000 [CFj]	-15'000 [CFi]	1 [ENTER] [↓]
15 [I/YR]	15 [i]	-12,000 [ENTER] [↓]
[ ] {NPV} -105,782	[NPV] -105'782	1 [ENTER] [↓]
		-13,000 [ENTER] [↓]
		1 [ENTER] [↓]
		-14,000 [ENTER] [↓]
		1 [ENTER] [↓]
		-15,000 [ENTER] [↓]
		1 [ENTER] [↓]
		[NPV]
		15 [ENTER]
		[↓] [CPT] -105,782

HP-10B	EL-733A	BA II Plus
-105,782 [PV]	-105'782 [PV]	-105,782 [PV]
6 [N]	6 [n]	6 [N]
15 [I/YR]	15 [i]	15 [I/Y]
[PMT] 27,952	[COMP] [PMT] 27'952	[CPT] [PMT] 27,952

Equivalent Annual Annuity: $- \$105{,}782 = X \cdot PVAF_{(15\%,\, 6)}$ $X = -\$27{,}951.51$

Assembly B

HP-10B	EL-733A	BA II Plus
-75,000 `CFj`	-75'000 `CFi`	`CF`
-5,000 `CFj`	-5'000 `CFi`	`2nd` {CLR Work}
-6,000 `CFj`	-6'000 `CFi`	-75,000 `ENTER` `↓`
-7,000 `CFj`	-7'000 `CFi`	-5,000 `ENTER` `↓`
-8,000 `CFj`	-8'000 `CFi`	1 `ENTER` `↓`
-9,000 `CFj`	-9'000 `CFi`	-6,000 `ENTER` `↓`
15 `I/YR`	15 `i`	1 `ENTER` `↓`
`☐` {NPV} -97,536	`NPV` -97'536	-7,000 `ENTER` `↓`
		1 `ENTER` `↓`
		-8,000 `ENTER` `↓`
		1 `ENTER` `↓`
		-9,000 `ENTER` `↓`
		1 `ENTER` `↓`
		`NPV`
		15 `ENTER`
		`↓` `CPT` -97,536

HP-10B	EL-733A	BA II Plus
-97,536 `PV`	-97'536 `PV`	-97,536 `PV`
5 `N`	5 `n`	5 `N`
15 `I/YR`	15 `i`	15 `I/Y`
`PMT` 29,096	`COMP` `PMT` 29'096	`CPT` `PMT` 29,096

Equivalent Annual Annuity: $-\$97{,}536 = X \cdot \text{PVAF}_{(15\%,\,5)}$ $X = -\$29{,}096.51$

Using the NPV criterion, Assembly B is preferred, because its NPV is less negative than Assembly A's. But this is incorrect! Use the equivalent annual annuity (EAA) approach to adjust for the projects' unequal lives. Choose **Assembly A** because its EAA of − $27,952 is less negative than Assembly B's EAA of − $29,096.

48. The most difficult part of this problem is determining the appropriate annual cash flows. The "benefits" of either project are reduced damages from flooding. Consequently,

Annual Net Benefits from Channel alternative

= Reduced damage – Island loss – Operating costs

= ($3.5 million - $750,000) – $25,000 – $275,000 = $2.45 million

Annual Net Benefits from Dam / Reservoir alternative

= Reduced damage – Farmland loss – Operating costs

= ($3.5 million - $300,000) – $60,000 – $350,000 = $2.79 million

Channel Alternative

HP-10B	EL-733A	BA II Plus
-12.50 [CF$_j$]	-12.50 [CF$_i$]	[CF]
2.45 [CF$_j$]	10.00 [2ndF] {N$_i$}	[2nd] {CLR Work}
10.00 [ ] {N$_j$}	2.45 [CF$_i$]	-12.50 [ENTER] [↓]
10.00 [I/YR]	10.00 [i]	2.45 [ENTER] [↓]
[ ] {NPV} 2.55	[NPV] 2.55	10.00 [ENTER] [↓]
		[NPV]
		10.00 [ENTER]
		[↓] [CPT] 2.55

Dam/Reservoir Alternative

HP-10B	EL-733A	BA II Plus	
-17.30 `CFj`	-17.30 `CFi`	`CF`	
2.79 `CFj`	14.00 `2ndF` {Ni}	`2nd` {CLR Work}	
14.00 `☐` {Nj}	2.79 `CFi`	-17.30 `ENTER` `↓`	
10.00 `I/YR`	10.00 `i`	2.79 `ENTER` `↓`	
`☐` {NPV} 3.25	`NPV` 3.25	14.00 `ENTER` `↓`	
		`NPV`	
		10.00 `ENTER`	
		`↓` `CPT` 3.25	

The net present value of the Channel proposal (rounded to the nearest .01 million) equals $2.55 million. The Dam/Reservoir proposal has a higher NPV of $3.25 million.

Using these numbers to solve for the equivalent annual annuities ...

Channel Alternative

HP-10B	EL-733A	BA II Plus
-2.55 `PV`	-2.55 `PV`	-2.55 `PV`
10.00 `I/YR`	10.00 `i`	10.00 `I/Y`
10.00 `N`	10.00 `n`	10.00 `N`
`PMT` 0.42	`COMP` `PMT` 0.42	`CPT` `PMT` 0.42

Equivalent Annual Annuity: $- \$2.55 \text{ million} = X \cdot \text{PVAF}_{(10\%, 10)}$

$X = \$0.42$ million

Dam/Reservoir Alternative

HP-10B	EL-733A	BA II Plus
-3.25 [PV]	-3.25 [PV]	-3.25 [PV]
10.00 [I/YR]	10.00 [i]	10.00 [I/Y]
14.00 [N]	14.00 [n]	14.00 [N]
[PMT] 0.44	[COMP] [PMT] 0.44	[CPT] [PMT] 0.44

Equivalent Annual Annuity: $- \$3.25 \text{ million} = X \cdot \text{PVAF}_{(10\%,\ 14)}$

X = \$0.44 million

The Dam/Reservoir proposal (EAA = \$0.44 million) maintains its advantage over the Channel alternative (EAA = \$0.42 million) when adjusted for the projects' unequal lives and is the superior choice. (Actually, this result was rather obvious. The Dam/Reservoir alternative had the higher NPV and a longer useful life.)

49. The value of the Phoenix's stock at t=3 can be determined using the dividend growth model.

The value of Phoenix's stock at t=3 equals $\dfrac{\$3.00(1.06)}{.14-.06} = \$39.75$

Using the information from the problem, we can re-write it in the form of a cash flow diagram:

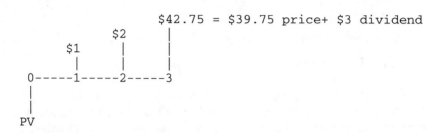

```
                              $42.75 = $39.75 price+ $3 dividend
                    $2          |
           $1        |          |
            |        |          |
    0-----1-----2-----3
    |
    |
   PV
```

HP-10B	**EL-733A**	**BA II Plus**
0.00 $\boxed{\text{CF}_j}$	0.00 $\boxed{\text{CF}_i}$	$\boxed{\text{CF}}$
1.00 $\boxed{\text{CF}_j}$	1.00 $\boxed{\text{CF}_i}$	$\boxed{\text{2nd}}$ {CLR Work}
2.00 $\boxed{\text{CF}_j}$	2.00 $\boxed{\text{CF}_i}$	0.00 $\boxed{\text{ENTER}}$ $\boxed{\downarrow}$
42.75 $\boxed{\text{CF}_j}$	42.75 $\boxed{\text{CF}_i}$	1.00 $\boxed{\text{ENTER}}$ $\boxed{\downarrow}$
14.00 $\boxed{\text{I/YR}}$	14.00 $\boxed{\text{i}}$	1 $\boxed{\text{ENTER}}$ $\boxed{\downarrow}$
$\boxed{}$ {NPV} 31.27	$\boxed{\text{NPV}}$ 31.27	2.00 $\boxed{\text{ENTER}}$ $\boxed{\downarrow}$
		1 $\boxed{\text{ENTER}}$ $\boxed{\downarrow}$
		42.75 $\boxed{\text{ENTER}}$ $\boxed{\downarrow}$
		1 $\boxed{\text{ENTER}}$ $\boxed{\downarrow}$
		$\boxed{\text{NPV}}$
		14.00 $\boxed{\text{ENTER}}$
		$\boxed{\downarrow}$ $\boxed{\text{CPT}}$ 31.27

The stock's current price should be $31.27.

50. First use the perpetuity formula to collapse the infinite series of cash flows beginning at t=5 to a single sum at t=4.

$$V_4 = \frac{\$500}{.10} = \$5,000$$

Next use the NPV function to determine the amount of "excess" cash at t=0.

HP-10B	EL-733A	BA II Plus	
-15,000 [CFj]	-15'000 [CFi]	[CF]	
3,000 [CFj]	3'000 [CFi]	[2nd] {CLR Work}	
0 [CFj]	0 [CFi]	-15,000 [ENTER] [↓]	
2,000 [CFj]	2'000 [CFi]	3,000 [ENTER] [↓]	
5,000 [CFj]	5'000 [CFi]	1 [ENTER] [↓]	
10 [I/YR]	10 [i]	0 [ENTER] [↓]	
□ {NPV} -7,355	[NPV] -7'355	1 [ENTER] [↓]	
		2,000 [ENTER] [↓]	
		1 [ENTER] [↓]	
		5,000 [ENTER] [↓]	
		1 [ENTER] [↓]	
		[NPV]	
		10 [ENTER]	
		[↓] [CPT] -7,355	

Finally use the TVM registers to obtain the cash flow at t=2 equivalent to the "excess" cash amount at t=0.

HP-10B	EL-733A	BA II Plus
-7,355 [PV]	-7'355 [PV]	-7,355 [PV]
2 [N]	2 [n]	2 [N]
10 [I/YR]	10 [i]	10 [I/Y]
[FV] 8,900	[COMP] [FV] 8'900	[CPT] [FV] 8,900

The unknown cash flow at t=2 equals $8,900.

51. The present value of the expected future cash flows can be valued as a growing perpetuity:

$$\text{Present value of future cash flows} = \frac{\$25,000}{.16 - .07} = \$277,777.78$$

Netting this figure against the $300,000 outlay yields a negative net present value of $22,222.22, so Yurdone should not start the cemetery business. The break-even growth rate must be solved for algebraically:

$$\$300,000 = \frac{\$25,000}{.16 - g} \qquad g \approx 7.67 \text{ percent}$$

52.

HP-10B		EL-733A		BA II Plus	
				2nd {Data}	
		2ndF {MODE}		2nd {CLR Work}	
1	Σ+	1	DATA *	1	ENTER ↓ ↓
0	Σ+	0	DATA	0	ENTER ↓ ↓
0	Σ+	0	DATA	0	ENTER ↓ ↓
1	Σ+	1	DATA	1	ENTER ↓ ↓
2	Σ+	2	DATA	2	ENTER ↓ ↓
1	Σ+	1	DATA	1	ENTER ↓ ↓
1	Σ+	1	DATA	1	ENTER ↓ ↓
0	Σ+	0	DATA	0	ENTER ↓ ↓
2	Σ+	2	DATA	2	ENTER ↓ ↓
1	Σ+	1	DATA	1	ENTER ↓ ↓
3	Σ+	3	DATA	3	ENTER ↓ ↓
☐ {x̄,ȳ}	1.0909	2ndF {x̄}	1.0909	2nd {Stat}	
☐ {Sx,Sy}	0.9439	2ndF {sx}	0.9439	2nd (SET) **	
				↓ ↓	1.0909
				↓	0.9439

* The M+ key becomes the DATA key in Statistics mode.

** Continue pressing 2nd {SET} until "1–V" is displayed for one-variable statistics.

The mean number $(\bar{x})$ of defective knives per 200-knife carton is 1.09; the sample standard deviation (s) equals 0.94 knives.

53.

HP-10B	EL-733A	BA II Plus
		2nd {Data}
	2ndF {MODE}	2nd {CLR Work}
95 Σ+	95 DATA *	95 ENTER ↓ ↓
90 Σ+	90 DATA	90 ENTER ↓ ↓
75 Σ+	75 DATA	75 ENTER ↓ ↓
82 Σ+	82 DATA	82 ENTER ↓ ↓
84 Σ+	84 DATA	84 ENTER ↓ ↓
86 Σ+	86 DATA	86 ENTER ↓ ↓
88 Σ+	88 DATA	88 ENTER ↓ ↓
55 Σ+	55 DATA	55 ENTER ↓ ↓
77 Σ+	77 DATA	77 ENTER ↓ ↓
63 Σ+	63 DATA	63 ENTER ↓ ↓
75 Σ+	75 DATA	75 ENTER ↓ ↓
85 Σ+	85 DATA	85 ENTER ↓ ↓
73 Σ+	73 DATA	73 ENTER ↓ ↓
99 Σ+	99 DATA	99 ENTER ↓ ↓
80 Σ+	80 DATA	80 ENTER ↓ ↓
92 Σ+	92 DATA	92 ENTER ↓ ↓
☐ {$\bar{x}, \bar{y}$} 81.19	2ndF {$\bar{x}$} 81.19	2nd {Stat}
☐ {$\sigma x, \sigma y$} 11.11	2ndF {σx} 11.11	2nd {SET} **
		↓ ↓ 81.19
		↓ ↓ 11.11

* The M+ key becomes the DATA key in Statistics mode.

** Continue pressing 2nd {SET} until "1–V" is displayed for one-variable statistics.

Because we have data on the entire population (Mr. Overstreet's COM 371 class), the population mean (μ) and standard deviation (σ) should be used. The population mean = 81.19 and the population standard deviation = 11.11.

54. $E(x) = .10(-5) + .70(12) + .20(30) = 13.90\,\%$

Hewlett-Packard HP-10B	**Sharp EL-733A**
-9.00 INPUT 0.10 Σ+	-9.00 (x,y) × 0.10 DATA
11.00 INPUT 0.70 Σ+	11.00 (x,y) × 0.70 DATA
28.00 INPUT 0.20 Σ+	29.00 (x,y) × 0.20 DATA
□ {x̄w} 12.40	2ndF {x̄} 12.40

Texas Instruments BA II Plus

2nd {Data} 2nd {CLR Work}

-9.00 ENTER ↓   10.00 ENTER ↓   *

11.00 ENTER ↓   70.00 ENTER ↓

28.00 ENTER ↓   20.00 ENTER ↓

2nd {Stat} 2nd {SET} **

↓ ↓ 12.40

*   When computing weighted averages, the BA II Plus requires all "weights" to be entered as whole numbers, NOT as decimal fractions.

**   Keep pressing 2nd {SET} until "1 - V" is displayed.

The expected return on this investment is 12.40 percent.

55. $E(x) = .60(11) + .25(17) + .15(31) = 15.50\%$

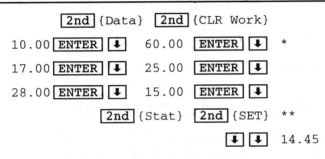

Hewlett-Packard HP-10B				Sharp EL-733A			
10.00 [INPUT]	0.60 [Σ+]			10.00 [(x,y)]	[×]	0.60 [DATA]	
17.00 [INPUT]	0.25 [Σ+]			17.00 [(x,y)]	[×]	0.25 [DATA]	
28.00 [INPUT]	0.15 [Σ+]			28.00 [(x,y)]	[×]	0.15 [DATA]	
	[ ] {x̄w} 14.45				[2ndF] {x̄} 14.45		

Texas Instruments BA II Plus

[2nd] {Data}   [2nd] {CLR Work}

10.00 [ENTER] [↓]   60.00 [ENTER] [↓]   *

17.00 [ENTER] [↓]   25.00 [ENTER] [↓]

28.00 [ENTER] [↓]   15.00 [ENTER] [↓]

[2nd] {Stat}   [2nd] {SET}   **

[↓] [↓]   14.45

* When computing weighted averages, the BA II Plus requires all "weights" to be entered as whole numbers, NOT as decimal fractions.

** Keep pressing [2nd] {SET} until "1 - V" is displayed.

Your portfolio's expected return is 14.45 percent.

56. The weighted average cost of capital is typically computed on an after-tax basis. Therefore, one must adjust the cost of debt to reflect the tax-deductibility of interest.

After-tax costs

After-tax cost of debt = $(8.00)(1 - .35) = 5.20$ percent

Preferred stock = 10.00 percent

Common stock = 15.00 percent

Without a financial calculator, it is necessary to determine the *weight* of financing source in the capital mix before computing the WACC:

Total capital = $20 million + $10 million + $50 million = $80 million

Weights

$$\text{Debt} = \$20/80 = 0.25$$

$$\text{Preferred stock} = \$10/80 = 0.125$$

$$\text{Common stock} = \$50/80 = 0.625$$

Weighted Average Cost of Capital

$$E(x) = .25(5.20) + .125(10) + .625(15) = 11.93\,\%$$

Financial calculators allow one to enter the weights directly:

Hewlett-Packard HP-10B	Sharp EL-733A
5.20 [INPUT] 20 [Σ+]	5.20 [(x,y)] [×] 20 [DATA]
10.00 [INPUT] 10 [Σ+]	10.00 [(x,y)] [×] 10 [DATA]
15.00 [INPUT] 50 [Σ+]	15.00 [(x,y)] [×] 50 [DATA]
[ ] {x̄w} 11.93	[2ndF] {x̄} 11.93

Texas Instruments BA II Plus

[2nd] {Data} [2nd] {CLR Work}

5.20 [ENTER] [↓] 20 [ENTER] [↓]

10.00 [ENTER] [↓] 10 [ENTER] [↓]

15.00 [ENTER] [↓] 50 [ENTER] [↓]

[2nd] {Stat} [2nd] {SET} **

[↓] [↓] 11.93

** Keep pressing [2nd] {SET} until "1 - V" is displayed.

Reactive Industries' after-tax weighted average cost of capital is 11.93 percent.

57. $E(x) = .20(2,400) + .30(4,800) + .40(6,000) + .10(7,200) = \$5,040$

Hewlett-Packard HP-10B	Sharp EL-733A
2,400 [INPUT] 0.20 [Σ+]	2'400 [(x,y)] [×] 0.20 [DATA]
4,800 [INPUT] 0.30 [Σ+]	4'800 [(x,y)] [×] 0.30 [DATA]
6,000 [INPUT] 0.40 [Σ+]	6'000 [(x,y)] [×] 0.40 [DATA]
7,200 [INPUT] 0.10 [Σ+]	7'200 [(x,y)] [×] 0.10 [DATA]
[ ] {x̄w} 5,040	[2ndF] {x̄} 5'040

Texas Instruments BA II Plus

[2nd] {Data} [2nd] {CLR Work}

2,400 [ENTER] [↓] 20.00* [ENTER] [↓]

4,800 [ENTER] [↓] 30.00 [ENTER] [↓]

6,000 [ENTER] [↓] 40.00 [ENTER] [↓]

7,200 [ENTER] [↓] 10.00 [ENTER] [↓]

[2nd] {Stat} [2nd] {SET} **

[↓] [↓] 5,040

* When computing weighted averages, the BA II Plus requires all "weights" to be entered as whole numbers, NOT as decimal fractions.

** Keep pressing [2nd] {SET} until "1 - V" is displayed.

HP-10B	EL-733A	BA II Plus
-20,000 [CFj]	-20'000 [CFi]	[CF]
5,040 [CFj]	5 [2ndF] {Ni}	[2nd] {CLR Work}
5 [ ] {Nj}	5'040 [CFi]	-20,000 [ENTER] [↓]
14 [I/YR]	14 [i]	5,040 [ENTER] [↓]
[ ] {NPV} -2,697	[NPV] -2'697	5 [ENTER] [↓]
		[NPV]
		14 [ENTER]
		[↓] [CPT] -2,697

Because the expected NPV of this investment is − $2,697, Larry should **not** buy the new equipment.

58.

Hewlett-Packard HP-10B

1,991 INPUT 40,000 Σ+

1,992 INPUT 43,000 Σ+

1,993 INPUT 47,000 Σ+

1,994 INPUT 45,000 Σ+

1,995 INPUT 50,000 Σ+

1,996 INPUT 55,000 Σ+

1,997 INPUT 65,000 Σ+

1,998 ☐ {$\hat{y}$, m} 63,857 <== 1998 sales

Sharp EL-733A

2ndF {MODE}

1'991 (x,y) 40'000 DATA

1'992 (x,y) 43'000 DATA

1'993 (x,y) 47'000 DATA

1'994 (x,y) 45'000 DATA

1'995 (x,y) 50'000 DATA

1'996 (x,y) 55'000 DATA

1'997 (x,y) 65'000 DATA

1'998 2ndF {y'} 63'857 <== 1998 sales

2nd {Data} 2nd {CLR Work}

1,991 ENTER ↓ 40,000 ENTER ↓

1,992 ENTER ↓ 43,000 ENTER ↓

1,993 ENTER ↓ 47,000 ENTER ↓

1,994 ENTER ↓ 45,000 ENTER ↓

1,995 ENTER ↓ 50,000 ENTER ↓

1,996 ENTER ↓ 55,000 ENTER ↓

1,997 ENTER ↓ 65,000 ENTER ↓

2nd {Stat} 2nd {SET} **

↓ ↓ ↓ ↓

↓ ↓ ↓ ↓

↓ ↓ ↓

1,998 ENTER

↓ CPT 63,857 <== predicted y

** Keep pressing 2nd {SET} until "LIN" is displayed.

Platypus Products' 1998 expected sales are $63,857.

59.

Hewlett-Packard HP-10B

-7.13 `INPUT` -8.21 `Σ+`

0.85 `INPUT` 1.64 `Σ+`

2.40 `INPUT` 1.61 `Σ+`

-2.73 `INPUT` -0.58 `Σ+`

8.80 `INPUT` 6.37 `Σ+`

-0.89 `INPUT` 1.29 `Σ+`

-0.52 `INPUT` -0.61 `Σ+`

-9.91 `INPUT` -6.98 `Σ+`

-5.25 `INPUT` -0.07 `Σ+`

-0.67 `INPUT` 3.87 `Σ+`

5.82 `INPUT` 4.06 `Σ+`

2.45 `INPUT` 2.04 `Σ+`

0 ☐ {$\hat{y}, \pi$} 0.7735 <== y-intercept

☐ {SWAP} 0.7157 <== slope (= beta)

Sharp EL-733A

`2ndF` {MODE}

-7.13 `(x,y)` -8.21 `DATA`

0.85 `(x,y)` 1.64 `DATA`

2.40 `(x,y)` 1.61 `DATA`

-2.73 `(x,y)` -0.58 `DATA`

8.80 `(x,y)` 6.37 `DATA`

-0.89 `(x,y)` 1.29 `DATA`

-0.52 `(x,y)` -0.61 `DATA`

-9.91 `(x,y)` -6.98 `DATA`

-5.25 `(x,y)` -0.07 `DATA`

-0.67 `(x,y)` 3.87 `DATA`

5.82 `(x,y)` 4.06 `DATA`

2.45 `(x,y)` 2.04 `DATA`

`2ndF` {a} 0.7735 <== y-intercept

`2ndF` {b} 0.7157 <== slope (= beta)

[2nd] {Data} [2nd] {CLR Work}

-7.13 [ENTER] [↓] -8.21 [ENTER] [↓]

0.85 [ENTER] [↓] 1.64 [ENTER] [↓]

2.40 [ENTER] [↓] 1.61 [ENTER] [↓]

-2.73 [ENTER] [↓] -0.58 [ENTER] [↓]

8.80 [ENTER] [↓] 6.37 [ENTER] [↓]

-0.89 [ENTER] [↓] 1.29 [ENTER] [↓]

-0.52 [ENTER] [↓] -0.61 [ENTER] [↓]

-9.91 [ENTER] [↓] -6.98 [ENTER] [↓]

-5.25 [ENTER] [↓] -0.07 [ENTER] [↓]

-0.67 [ENTER] [↓] 3.87 [ENTER] [↓]

5.82 [ENTER] [↓] 4.06 [ENTER] [↓]

2.45 [ENTER] [↓] 2.04 [ENTER] [↓]

[2nd] {Stat} [2nd] {SET}

[↓] [↓] [↓] [↓]

[↓] [↓] [↓] [↓] 0.7735 <== y-intercept

[↓] 0.7157 <== slope (= beta)

** Keep pressing [2nd] {SET} until "LIN" is displayed.

Whiz-Bang has a beta coefficient of 0.72.

Hewlett-Packard HP-10B

1,983 INPUT 2,338 Σ+

1,984 INPUT 1,728 Σ+

1,985 INPUT 1,331 Σ+

1,986 INPUT 735 Σ+

1,987 INPUT 580 Σ+

1,988 INPUT 569 Σ+

1,989 INPUT 274 Σ+

1,990 INPUT 539 Σ+

1,991 INPUT 438 Σ+

1,992 INPUT 356 Σ+

0 ☐ {x̂,r } 1992.05 <== predicted x

☐ {SWAP} -0.86 <== r

Sharp EL-733A

2ndF {MODE}

1'983 (x,y) 2'338 DATA

1'984 (x,y) 1'728 DATA

1'985 (x,y) 1'331 DATA

1'986 (x,y) 735 DATA

1'987 (x,y) 580 DATA

1'988 (x,y) 569 DATA

1'989 (x,y) 274 DATA

1'990 (x,y) 539 DATA

1'991 (x,y) 438 DATA

1'992 (x,y) 356 DATA

0 2ndF {x'} 1992.05 <== predicted x

2ndF {r} -0.86 <== r

[2nd] {Data}   [2nd] {CLR Work}

1,983 [ENTER] [↓]   2,338 [ENTER] [↓]

1,984 [ENTER] [↓]   1,728 [ENTER] [↓]

1,985 [ENTER] [↓]   1,331 [ENTER] [↓]

1,986 [ENTER] [↓]   735 [ENTER] [↓]

1,987 [ENTER] [↓]   580 [ENTER] [↓]

1,988 [ENTER] [↓]   569 [ENTER] [↓]

1,989 [ENTER] [↓]   274 [ENTER] [↓]

1,990 [ENTER] [↓]   539 [ENTER] [↓]

1,991 [ENTER] [↓]   438 [ENTER] [↓]

1,992 [ENTER] [↓]   356 [ENTER] [↓]

[2nd] {Stat}   [2nd] {SET}

[↓] [↓] [↓] [↓]

[↓] [↓] [↓] [↓]

[↓] [↓] [↓] [↓]

0 [ENTER]

[↑] [CPT]   1,992.05   <== predicted x

** Keep pressing [2nd] {SET} until "LIN" is displayed.

Assuming the data is correct and the annual bay scallop catch is linearly related to time, the last bay scallop should have been caught at time t=1992.05, or about 18 days into the year 1992. This seems rather unlikely, and illustrates the dangers of using simple linear models to forecast complex phenomena.

BIBLIOGRAPHY

Block, S. and G. Hirt. *Foundations of Financial Management, 9th Ed.*, (Burr Ridge, IL: Irwin/McGraw-Hill, 2000).

Brealey, R. A., S. C. Myers, and A. J. Marcus. *Fundamentals of Corporate Finance, 2nd Ed.*, (Burr Ridge, IL: Irwin/McGraw-Hill, 1999).

Brigham, E. and J. Houston. *Fundamentals of Financial Management, 9th Ed.*, (Fort Worth, TX: The Dryden Press, 1998).

Emery, D., J. Finnerty and J. Stone. *Principles of Financial Management*, (Upper Saddle River, NJ: Prentice-Hall, 1998).

Gitman, L. *Principles of Managerial Finance, 8th Ed.*, (New York: Addison-Wesley Publishers, 2000).

Hewlett-Packard Corporation. *HP-10B Business Calculator: Owner's Manual, Ed. 1.*, (Canada: Hewlett-Packard, November 1988).

Keown, A., D. Scott, J. Martin and J. W. Petty. *Foundations of Finance*, 2nd Ed., (Upper Saddle River, NJ: Prentice-Hall, 1998).

Moyer, R. C., J. R. McGuigan and W. J. Kretlow. *Contemporary Financial Management, 7th Ed.*, (St. Paul, MN: West Publishing Company, 1998).

Ross, S., R. Westerfield and B. Jordan. *Essentials of Corporate Finance, 2nd Ed.* (Burr Ridge, IL: Irwin/McGraw-Hill, 1999).

Ross, S., R. Westerfield and B. Jordan. *Fundamentals of Corporate Finance, 5th Ed.*, (Burr Ridge, IL: Irwin/McGraw-Hill, 2000).

Sharp Electronics Corporation. *The SHARP EL-733A Financial Calculator*, (Taiwan: Sharp Electronics Corporation, 1992).

Texas Instruments Instructional Communications. *BA II Plus Guidebook*, (Italy: Texas Instruments, Inc., 1991).

Van Horne, J. C. and J. M. Wachowicz, Jr. *Fundamentals of Financial Management, 10th Ed.*, (Englewood Cliffs, NJ: Prentice-Hall, 1998).

Weston, F., S. Besley and E. Brigham. *Essentials of Financial Management, 11th Ed.*, (Fort Worth, TX: The Dryden Press, 1999).

White, M. A. "Financial Problem-Solving with an Electronic Calculator," *Financial Practice and Education* (Fall 1991), pp. 73-88.

White, M. A. "Financial Problem-Solving with an Electronic Calculator: Texas Instruments' BA II Plus," *Financial Practice and Education* (Fall 1993), pp. 123-126.

Appendix A

SUMMARY OF CASH FLOW DIAGRAMS

Present or Future Value of a Single Sum

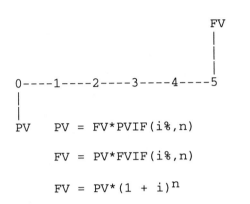

$$PV = FV*PVIF(i\%,n)$$

$$FV = PV*FVIF(i\%,n)$$

$$FV = PV*(1 + i)^n$$

"Annuity with a Tail"

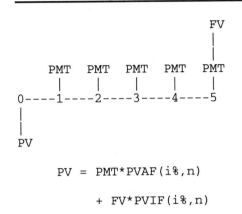

$$PV = PMT*PVAF(i\%,n)$$

$$+ FV*PVIF(i\%,n)$$

Future Value of an Annuity

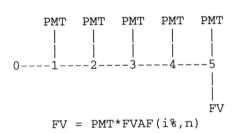

$$FV = PMT*FVAF(i\%,n)$$

Present Value of an Annuity

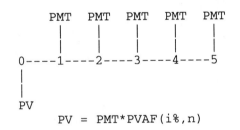

$$PV = PMT*PVAF(i\%,n)$$

Perpetuity

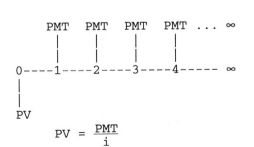

$$PV = \frac{PMT}{i}$$

Constant Growth Perpetuity

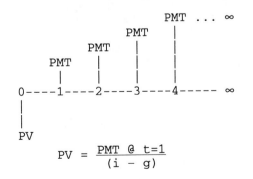

$$PV = \frac{PMT \ @ \ t=1}{(i - g)}$$

Appendix B

PRESENT VALUE/FUTURE VALUE TABLES

Table B.1   Future Value Interest Factor $= \mathrm{FVIF}_{(i\%, n)} = (1 + i)^n$

Future value of \$1 at the end of n periods

					Interest rate				
Period	1%	2%	3%	4%	5%	6%	7%	8%	9%
1	1.0100	1.0200	1.0300	1.0400	1.0500	1.0600	1.0700	1.0800	1.0900
2	1.0201	1.0404	1.0609	1.0816	1.1025	1.1236	1.1449	1.1664	1.1881
3	1.0303	1.0612	1.0927	1.1249	1.1576	1.1910	1.2250	1.2597	1.2950
4	1.0406	1.0824	1.1255	1.1699	1.2155	1.2625	1.3108	1.3605	1.4116
5	1.0510	1.1041	1.1593	1.2167	1.2763	1.3382	1.4026	1.4693	1.5386
6	1.0615	1.1262	1.1941	1.2653	1.3401	1.4185	1.5007	1.5869	1.6771
7	1.0721	1.1487	1.2299	1.3159	1.4071	1.5036	1.6058	1.7138	1.8280
8	1.0829	1.1717	1.2668	1.3686	1.4775	1.5938	1.7182	1.8509	1.9926
9	1.0937	1.1951	1.3048	1.4233	1.5513	1.6895	1.8385	1.9990	2.1719
10	1.1046	1.2190	1.3439	1.4802	1.6289	1.7908	1.9672	2.1589	2.3674
11	1.1157	1.2434	1.3842	1.5395	1.7103	1.8983	2.1049	2.3316	2.5804
12	1.1268	1.2682	1.4258	1.6010	1.7959	2.0122	2.2522	2.5182	2.8127
13	1.1381	1.2936	1.4685	1.6651	1.8856	2.1329	2.4098	2.7196	3.0658
14	1.1495	1.3195	1.5126	1.7317	1.9799	2.2609	2.5785	2.9372	3.3417
15	1.1610	1.3459	1.5580	1.8009	2.0789	2.3966	2.7590	3.1722	3.6425
16	1.1726	1.3728	1.6047	1.8730	2.1829	2.5404	2.9522	3.4259	3.9703
17	1.1843	1.4002	1.6528	1.9479	2.2920	2.6928	3.1588	3.7000	4.3276
18	1.1961	1.4282	1.7024	2.0258	2.4066	2.8543	3.3799	3.9960	4.7171
19	1.2081	1.4568	1.7535	2.1068	2.5270	3.0256	3.6165	4.3157	5.1417
20	1.2202	1.4859	1.8061	2.1911	2.6533	3.2071	3.8697	4.6610	5.6044
21	1.2324	1.5157	1.8603	2.2788	2.7860	3.3996	4.1406	5.0338	6.1088
22	1.2447	1.5460	1.9161	2.3699	2.9253	3.6035	4.4304	5.4365	6.6586
23	1.2572	1.5769	1.9736	2.4647	3.0715	3.8197	4.7405	5.8715	7.2579
24	1.2697	1.6084	2.0328	2.5633	3.2251	4.0489	5.0724	6.3412	7.9111
25	1.2824	1.6406	2.0938	2.6658	3.3864	4.2919	5.4274	6.8485	8.6231
30	1.3478	1.8114	2.4273	3.2434	4.3219	5.7435	7.6123	10.063	13.268
40	1.4889	2.2080	3.2620	4.8010	7.0400	10.286	14.974	21.725	31.409
50	1.6446	2.6916	4.3839	7.1067	11.467	18.420	29.457	46.902	74.358
60	1.8167	3.2810	5.8916	10.520	18.679	32.988	57.946	101.26	176.03

Table B.1 Future Value Interest Factor $= \text{FVIF}_{(i\%, n)} = (1 + i)^n$

(concluded) Future value of $1 at the end of n periods

					Interest rate					
10%	12%	14%	15%	16%	18%	20%	24%	28%	32%	36%
1.1000	1.1200	1.1400	1.1500	1.1600	1.1800	1.2000	1.2400	1.2800	1.3200	1.3600
1.2100	1.2544	1.2996	1.3225	1.3456	1.3924	1.4400	1.5376	1.6384	1.7424	1.8496
1.3310	1.4049	1.4815	1.5209	1.5609	1.6430	1.7280	1.9066	2.0972	2.3000	2.5155
1.4641	1.5735	1.6890	1.7490	1.8106	1.9388	2.0736	2.3642	2.6844	3.0360	3.4210
1.6105	1.7623	1.9254	2.0114	2.1003	2.2878	2.4883	2.9316	3.4360	4.0075	4.6526
1.7716	1.9738	2.1950	2.3131	2.4364	2.6996	2.9860	3.6352	4.3980	5.2899	6.3275
1.9487	2.2107	2.5023	2.6600	2.8262	3.1855	3.5832	4.5077	5.6295	6.9826	8.6054
2.1436	2.4760	2.8526	3.0590	3.2784	3.7589	4.2998	5.5895	7.2058	9.2170	11.703
2.3579	2.7731	3.2519	3.5179	3.8030	4.4355	5.1598	6.9310	9.2234	12.166	15.917
2.5937	3.1058	3.7072	4.0456	4.4114	5.2338	6.1917	8.5944	11.806	16.060	21.647
2.8531	3.4785	4.2262	4.6524	5.1173	6.1759	7.4301	10.657	15.112	21.199	29.439
3.1384	3.8960	4.8179	5.3503	5.9360	7.2876	8.9161	13.215	19.343	27.983	40.037
3.4523	4.3635	5.4924	6.1528	6.8858	8.5994	10.699	16.386	24.759	36.937	54.451
3.7975	4.8871	6.2613	7.0757	7.9875	10.147	12.839	20.319	31.691	48.757	74.053
4.1772	5.4736	7.1379	8.1371	9.2655	11.974	15.407	25.196	40.565	64.359	100.71
4.5950	6.1304	8.1372	9.3576	10.748	14.129	18.488	31.243	51.923	84.954	136.97
5.0545	6.8660	9.2765	10.761	12.468	16.672	22.186	38.741	66.461	112.14	186.28
5.5599	7.6900	10.575	12.375	14.463	19.673	26.623	48.039	85.071	148.02	253.34
6.1159	8.6128	12.056	14.232	16.777	23.214	31.948	59.568	108.89	195.39	344.54
6.7275	9.6463	13.743	16.367	19.461	27.393	38.338	73.864	139.38	257.92	468.57
7.4002	10.804	15.668	18.822	22.574	32.324	46.005	91.592	178.41	340.45	637.26
8.1403	12.100	17.861	21.645	26.186	38.142	55.206	113.57	228.36	449.39	866.67
8.9543	13.552	20.362	24.891	30.376	45.008	66.247	140.83	292.30	593.20	1178.7
9.8497	15.179	23.212	28.625	35.236	53.109	79.497	174.63	374.14	783.02	1603.0
10.835	17.000	26.462	32.919	40.874	62.669	95.396	216.54	478.90	1033.6	2180.1
17.449	29.960	50.950	66.212	85.850	143.37	237.38	634.82	1645.5	4142.1	10143.
45.259	93.051	188.88	267.86	378.72	750.38	1469.8	5455.9	19427.	66521.	*
117.39	289.00	700.23	1083.7	1670.7	3927.4	9100.4	46890.	*	*	*
304.48	897.60	2595.9	4384.0	7370.2	20555.	56348.	*	*	*	*

*The factor is greater than 99.999.

Table B.2 Present Value Interest Factor = $PVIF_{(i\%, n)} = \dfrac{1}{(1+i)^n}$

Present value of \$1 to be received after n periods

Interest rate

Period	1%	2%	3%	4%	5%	6%	7%	8%	9%
1	0.9901	0.9804	0.9709	0.9615	0.9524	0.9434	0.9346	0.9259	0.9174
2	0.9803	0.9612	0.9426	0.9246	0.9070	0.8900	0.8734	0.8573	0.8417
3	0.9706	0.9423	0.9151	0.8890	0.8638	0.8396	0.8163	0.7938	0.7722
4	0.9610	0.9238	0.8885	0.8548	0.8227	0.7921	0.7629	0.7350	0.7084
5	0.9515	0.9057	0.8626	0.8219	0.7835	0.7473	0.7130	0.6806	0.6499
6	0.9420	0.8880	0.8375	0.7903	0.7462	0.7050	0.6663	0.6302	0.5963
7	0.9327	0.8706	0.8131	0.7599	0.7107	0.6651	0.6227	0.5835	0.5470
8	0.9235	0.8535	0.7894	0.7307	0.6768	0.6274	0.5820	0.5403	0.5019
9	0.9143	0.8368	0.7664	0.7026	0.6446	0.5919	0.5439	0.5002	0.4604
10	0.9053	0.8203	0.7441	0.6756	0.6139	0.5584	0.5083	0.4632	0.4224
11	0.8963	0.8043	0.7224	0.6496	0.5847	0.5268	0.4751	0.4289	0.3875
12	0.8874	0.7885	0.7014	0.6246	0.5568	0.4970	0.4440	0.3971	0.3555
13	0.8787	0.7730	0.6810	0.6006	0.5303	0.4688	0.4150	0.3677	0.3262
14	0.8700	0.7579	0.6611	0.5775	0.5051	0.4423	0.3878	0.3405	0.2992
15	0.8613	0.7430	0.6419	0.5553	0.4810	0.4173	0.3624	0.3152	0.2745
16	0.8528	0.7284	0.6232	0.5339	0.4581	0.3936	0.3387	0.2919	0.2519
17	0.8444	0.7142	0.6050	0.5134	0.4363	0.3714	0.3166	0.2703	0.2311
18	0.8360	0.7002	0.5874	0.4936	0.4155	0.3503	0.2959	0.2502	0.2120
19	0.8277	0.6864	0.5703	0.4746	0.3957	0.3305	0.2765	0.2317	0.1945
20	0.8195	0.6730	0.5537	0.4564	0.3769	0.3118	0.2584	0.2145	0.1784
21	0.8114	0.6598	0.5375	0.4388	0.3589	0.2942	0.2415	0.1987	0.1637
22	0.8034	0.6468	0.5219	0.4220	0.3418	0.2775	0.2257	0.1839	0.1502
23	0.7954	0.6342	0.5067	0.4057	0.3256	0.2618	0.2109	0.1703	0.1378
24	0.7876	0.6217	0.4919	0.3901	0.3101	0.2470	0.1971	0.1577	0.1264
25	0.7798	0.6095	0.4776	0.3751	0.2953	0.2330	0.1842	0.1460	0.1160
30	0.7419	0.5521	0.4120	0.3083	0.2314	0.1741	0.1314	0.0994	0.0754
40	0.6717	0.4529	0.3066	0.2083	0.1420	0.0972	0.0668	0.0460	0.0318
50	0.6080	0.3715	0.2281	0.1407	0.0872	0.0543	0.0339	0.0213	0.0134

Table B.2   Present Value Interest Factor = $PVIF_{(i\%, n)} = \dfrac{1}{(1+i)^n}$

(concluded)   Present value of $1 to be received after n periods

Interest rate

10%	12%	14%	15%	16%	18%	20%	24%	28%	32%	36%
0.9091	0.8929	0.8772	0.8696	0.8621	0.8475	0.8333	0.8065	0.7813	0.7576	0.7353
0.8264	0.7972	0.7695	0.7561	0.7432	0.7182	0.6944	0.6504	0.6104	0.5739	0.5407
0.7513	0.7118	0.6750	0.6575	0.6407	0.6086	0.5787	0.5245	0.4768	0.4348	0.3975
0.6830	0.6355	0.5921	0.5718	0.5523	0.5158	0.4823	0.4230	0.3725	0.3294	0.2923
0.6209	0.5674	0.5194	0.4972	0.4761	0.4371	0.4019	0.3411	0.2910	0.2495	0.2149
0.5645	0.5066	0.4556	0.4323	0.4104	0.3704	0.3349	0.2751	0.2274	0.1890	0.1580
0.5132	0.4523	0.3996	0.3759	0.3538	0.3139	0.2791	0.2218	0.1776	0.1432	0.1162
0.4665	0.4039	0.3506	0.3269	0.3050	0.2660	0.2326	0.1789	0.1388	0.1085	0.0854
0.4241	0.3606	0.3075	0.2843	0.2630	0.2255	0.1938	0.1443	0.1084	0.0822	0.0628
0.3855	0.3220	0.2697	0.2472	0.2267	0.1911	0.1615	0.1164	0.0847	0.0623	0.0462
0.3505	0.2875	0.2366	0.2149	0.1954	0.1619	0.1346	0.0938	0.0662	0.0472	0.0340
0.3186	0.2567	0.2076	0.1869	0.1685	0.1372	0.1122	0.0757	0.0517	0.0357	0.0250
0.2897	0.2292	0.1821	0.1625	0.1452	0.1163	0.0935	0.0610	0.0404	0.0271	0.0184
0.2633	0.2046	0.1597	0.1413	0.1252	0.0985	0.0779	0.0492	0.0316	0.0205	0.0135
0.2394	0.1827	0.1401	0.1229	0.1079	0.0835	0.0649	0.0397	0.0247	0.0155	0.0099
0.2176	0.1631	0.1229	0.1069	0.0930	0.0708	0.0541	0.0320	0.0193	0.0118	0.0073
0.1978	0.1456	0.1078	0.0929	0 0802	0.0600	0.0451	0.0258	0.0150	0.0089	0.0054
0.1799	0.1300	0.0946	0.0808	0.0691	0.0508	0.0376	0.0208	0.0118	0.0068	0.0039
0.1635	0.1161	0.0829	0.0703	0.0596	0.0431	0.0313	0.0168	0.0092	0.0051	0.0029
0.1486	0.1037	0.0728	0.0611	0.0514	0.0365	0.0261	0.0135	0.0072	0.0039	0.0021
0.1351	0.0926	0.0638	0.0531	0.0443	0.0309	0.0217	0.0109	0.0056	0.0029	0.0016
0.1228	0.0826	0.0560	0.0462	0.0382	0.0262	0.0181	0.0088	0.0044	0.0022	0.0012
0.1117	0.0738	0.0491	0.0402	0.0329	0.0222	0.0151	0.0071	0.0034	0.0017	0.0008
0.1015	0.0659	0.0431	0.0349	0.0284	0.0188	0.0126	0.0057	0.0027	0.0013	0.0006
0.0923	0.0588	0.0378	0.0304	0.0245	0.0160	0.0105	0.0046	0.0021	0.0010	0.0005
0.0573	0.0334	0.0196	0.0151	0.0116	0.0070	0.0042	0.0016	0.0006	0.0002	0.0001
0.0221	0.0107	0.0053	0.0037	0.0026	0.0013	0.0007	0.0002	0.0001	*	*
0.0085	0.0035	0.0014	0.0009	0.0006	0.0003	0.0001	*	*	*	*

*The factor is zero to four decimal places.

Table B.3 Future Value Annuity Factor = $FVAF_{(i\%, n)} = \left[\dfrac{(1+i)^n - 1}{i}\right]$

Future value of an annuity of $1 per period for n periods

Number of periods	Interest rate								
	1%	2%	3%	4%	5%	6%	7%	8%	9%
1	1.0000	1.0000	1.0000	1.0000	1.0000	1.0000	1.0000	1.0000	1.0000
2	2.0100	2.0200	2.0300	2.0400	2.0500	2.0600	2.0700	2.0800	2.0900
3	3.0301	3.0604	3.0909	3.1216	3.1525	3.1836	3.2149	3.2464	3.2781
4	4.0604	4.1216	4.1836	4.2465	4.3101	4.3746	4.4399	4.5061	4.5731
5	5.1010	5.2040	5.3091	5.4163	5.5256	5.6371	5.7507	5.8666	5.9847
6	6.1520	6.3081	6.4684	6.6330	6.8019	6.9753	7.1533	7.3359	7.5233
7	7.2135	7.4343	7.6625	7.8983	8.1420	8.3938	8.6540	8.9228	9.2004
8	8.2857	8.5830	8.8932	9.2142	9.5491	9.8975	10.260	10.637	11.028
9	9.3685	9.7546	10.159	10.583	11.027	11.491	11.978	12.488	13.021
10	10.462	10.950	11.464	12.006	12.578	13.181	13.816	14.487	15.193
11	11.567	12.169	12.808	13.486	14.207	14.972	15.784	16.645	17.560
12	12.683	13.412	14.192	15.026	15.917	16.870	17.888	18.977	20.141
13	13.809	14.680	15.618	16.627	17.713	18.882	20.141	21.495	22.953
14	14.947	15.974	17.086	18.292	19.599	21.015	22.550	24.215	26.019
15	16.097	17.293	18.599	20.024	21.579	23.276	25.129	27.152	29.361
16	17.258	18.639	20.157	21.825	23.657	25.673	27.888	30.324	33.003
17	18.430	20.012	21.762	23.698	25.840	28.213	30.840	33.750	36.974
18	19.615	21.412	23.414	25.645	28.132	30.906	33.999	37.450	41.301
19	20.811	22.841	25.117	27.671	30.539	33.760	37.379	41.446	46.018
20	22.019	24.297	26.870	29.778	33.066	36.786	40.995	45.762	51.160
21	23.239	25.783	28.676	31.969	35.719	39.993	44.865	50.423	56.765
22	24.472	27.299	30.537	34.248	38.505	43.392	49.006	55.457	62.873
23	25.716	28.845	32.453	36.618	41.430	46.996	53.436	60.893	69.532
24	26.973	30.422	34.426	39.083	44.502	50.816	58.177	66.765	76.790
25	28.243	32.030	36.459	41.646	47.727	54.865	63.249	73.106	84.701
30	34.785	40.568	47.575	56.085	66.439	79.058	94.461	113.28	136.31
40	48.886	60.402	75.401	95.026	120.80	154.76	199.64	259.06	337.88
50	64.463	84.579	112.80	152.67	209.35	290.34	406.53	573.77	815.08
60	81.670	114.05	163.05	237.99	353.58	533.13	813.52	1253.2	1944.8

Table B.3 Future Value Annuity Factor = $FVAF_{(i\%, n)} = \left[\dfrac{(1+i)^n - 1}{i}\right]$

(concluded) Future value of an annuity of $1 per period for n periods

					Interest rate					
10%	12%	14%	15%	16%	18%	20%	24%	28%	32%	36%
1.0000	1.0000	1.0000	1.0000	1.0000	1.0000	1.0000	1.0000	1.0000	1.0000	1.0000
2.1000	2.1200	2.1400	2.1500	2.1600	2.1800	2.2000	2.2400	2.2800	2.3200	2.3600
3.3100	3.3744	3.4396	3.4725	3.5056	3.5724	3.6400	3.7776	3.9184	4.0624	4.2096
4.6410	4.7793	4.9211	4.9934	5.0665	5.2154	5.3680	5.6842	6.0156	6.3624	6.7251
6.1051	6.3528	6.6101	6.7424	6.8771	7.1542	7.4416	8.0484	8.6999	9.3983	10.146
7.7156	8.1152	8.5355	8.7537	8.9775	9.4420	9.9299	10.980	12.136	13.406	14.799
9.4872	10.629	10.730	11.067	11.414	12.142	12.916	14.615	16.534	18.696	21.126
11.436	12.300	13.233	13.727	14.240	15.327	16.499	19.123	22.163	25.678	29.732
13.579	14.776	16.085	16.786	17.519	19.086	20.799	24.712	29.369	34.895	41.435
15.937	17.549	19.337	20.304	21.321	23.521	25.959	31.643	38.593	47.062	57.352
18.531	20.655	23.045	24.349	25.733	28.755	32.150	40.238	50.398	63.122	78.998
21.384	24.133	27.271	29.002	30.850	34.931	39.581	50.895	65.510	84.320	108.44
24.523	28.029	32.089	34.352	36.786	42.219	48.497	64.110	84.853	112.30	148.47
27.975	32.393	37.581	40.505	43.672	50.818	59.196	80.496	109.61	149.24	202.93
31.772	37.280	43.842	47.580	51.660	60.965	72.035	100.82	141.30	198.00	276.98
35.950	42.753	50.980	55.717	60.925	72.939	87.442	126.01	181.87	262.36	377.69
40.545	48.884	59.118	65.075	71.673	87.068	105.93	157.25	233.79	347.31	514.66
45.599	55.750	68.394	75.836	84.141	103.74	128.12	195.99	300.25	459.45	700.94
51.159	63.440	78.969	88.212	98.603	123.41	154.74	244.03	385.32	607.47	954.28
57.275	72.052	91.025	102.44	115.38	146.63	186.69	303.60	494.21	802.86	1298.8
64.002	81.699	104.77	118.81	134.84	174.02	225.03	377.46	633.59	1060.8	1767.4
71.403	92.503	120.44	137.63	157.41	206.34	271.03	469.06	812.00	1401.2	2404.7
79.543	104.60	138.30	159.28	183.60	244.49	326.24	582.63	1040.4	1850.6	3271.3
88.497	118.16	158.66	184.17	213.98	289.49	392.48	723.46	1332.7	2443.8	4450.0
98.347	133.33	181.87	212.79	249.21	342.60	471.98	898.09	1706.8	3226.8	6053.0
164.49	241.33	356.79	434.75	530.31	790.95	1181.9	2640.9	5873.2	12941.	28172.3
442.59	767.09	1342.0	1779.1	2360.8	4163.2	7343.9	22729.	69377.	*	*
1163.9	2400.0	4994.5	7217.7	10436.	21813.	45497.	*	*	*	*
3034.8	7471.6	18535.	29220.	46058.	*	*	*	*	*	*

*The factor is greater than 99,999.

Table B.4 Present Value Annuity Factor = $PVAF_{(i\%, n)} = \left[\dfrac{1 - \dfrac{1}{(1+i)^n}}{i} \right]$

Present value of an annuity of $1 per period for n periods

Number of periods	Interest rate								
	1%	2%	3%	4%	5%	6%	7%	8%	9%
1	0.9901	0.9804	0.9709	0.9615	0.9524	0.9434	0.9346	0.9259	0.9174
2	1.9704	1.9416	1.9135	1.8861	1.8594	1.8334	1.8080	1.7833	1.7591
3	2.9410	2.8839	2.8286	2.7751	2.7232	2.6730	2.6243	2.5771	2.5313
4	3.9020	3.8077	3.7171	3.6299	3.5460	3.4651	3.3872	3.3121	3.2397
5	4.8534	4.7135	4.5797	4.4518	4.3295	4.2124	4.1002	3.9927	3.8897
6	5.7955	5.6014	5.4172	5.2421	5.0757	4.9173	4.7665	4.6229	4.4859
7	6.7282	6.4720	6.2303	6.0021	5.7864	5.5824	5.3893	5.2064	5.0330
8	7.6517	7.3255	7.0197	6.7327	6.4632	6.2098	5.9713	5.7466	5.5348
9	8.5660	8.1622	7.7861	7.4353	7.1078	6.8017	6.5152	6.2469	5.9952
10	9.4713	8.9826	8.5302	8.1109	7.7217	7.3601	7.0236	6.7101	6.4177
11	10.3676	9.7868	9.2526	8.7605	8.3064	7.8869	7.4987	7.1390	6.8052
12	11.2551	10.5753	9.9540	9.3851	8.8633	8.3838	7.9427	7.5361	7.1607
13	12.1337	11.3484	10.6350	9.9856	9.3936	8.8527	8.3577	7.9038	7.4869
14	13.0037	12.1062	11.2961	10.5631	9.8986	9.2950	8.7455	8.2442	7.7862
15	13.8651	12.8493	11.9379	11.1184	10.3797	9.7122	9.1079	8.5595	8.0607
16	14.7179	13.5777	12.5611	11.6523	10.8378	10.1059	9.4466	8.8514	8.3126
17	15.5623	14.2919	13.1661	12.1657	11.2741	10.4773	9.7632	9.1216	8.5436
18	16.3983	14.9920	13.7535	12.6593	11.6896	10.8276	10.0591	9.3719	8.7556
19	17.2260	15.6785	14.3238	13.1339	12.0853	11.1581	10.3356	9.6036	8.9501
20	18.0456	16.3514	14.8775	13.5903	12.4622	11.4699	10.5940	9.8181	9.1285
21	18.8570	17.0112	15.4150	14.0292	12.8212	11.7641	10.8355	10.0168	9.2922
22	19.6604	17.6580	15.9369	14.4511	13.1630	12.0416	11.0612	10.2007	9.4424
23	20.4558	18.2922	16.4436	14.8568	13.4886	12.3034	11.2722	10.3741	9.5802
24	21.2434	18.9139	16.9355	15.2470	13.7986	12.5504	11.4693	10.5288	9.7066
25	22.0232	19.5235	17.4131	15.6221	14.0939	12.7834	11.6536	10.6748	9.8226
30	25.8077	22.3965	19.6004	17.2920	15.3725	13.7648	12.4090	11.2578	10.2737
40	32.8347	27.3555	23.1148	19.7928	17.1591	15.0463	13.3317	11.9246	10.7574
50	39.1961	31.4236	25.7298	21.4822	18.2559	15.7619	13.8007	12.2335	10.9617

Table B.4 Present Value Annuity Factor = $\text{PVAF}_{(i\%,\,n)} = \left[\dfrac{1 - \dfrac{1}{(1+i)^n}}{i}\right]$

(concluded) Present value of an annuity of $1 per period for n periods

					Interest rate				
10%	12%	14%	15%	..16%	18%	20%	24%	28%	32%
0.9091	0.8929	0.8772	0.8696	0.8621	0.8475	0.8333	0.8065	0.7813	0.7576
1.7355	1.6901	1.6467	1.6257	1.6052	1.5656	1.5278	1.4568	1.3916	1.3315
2.4869	2.4018	2.3216	2.2832	2.2459	2.1743	2.1065	1.9813	1.8684	1.7663
3.1699	3.0373	2.9137	2.8550	2.7982	2.6901	2.5887	2.4043	2.2410	2.0957
3.7908	3.6048	3.4331	3.3522	3.2743	3.1272	2.9906	2.7454	2.5320	2.3452
4.3553	4.1114	3.8887	3.7845	3.6847	3.4976	3.3255	3.0205	2.7594	2.5342
4.8684	4.5638	4.2883	4.1604	4.0386	3.8115	3.6046	3.2423	2.9370	2.6775
5.3349	4.9676	4.6389	4.4873	4.3436	4.0776	3.8372	3.4212	3.0758	2.7860
5.7590	5.3282	4.9464	4.7716	4.6065	4.3030	4.0310	3.5655	3.1842	2.8681
6.1446	5.6502	5.2161	5.0188	4.8332	4.4941	4.1925	3.6819	3.2689	2.9304
6.4951	5.9377	5.4527	5.2337	5.0286	4.6560	4.3271	3.7757	3.3351	2.9776
6.8137	6.1944	5.6603	5.4206	5.1971	4.7932	4.4392	3.8514	3.3868	3.0133
7.1034	6.4235	5.8424	5.5831	5.3423	4.9095	4.5327	3.9124	3.4272	3.0404
7.3667	6.6282	6.0021	5.7245	5.4675	5.0081	4.6106	3.9616	3.4587	3.0609
7.6061	6.8109	6.1422	5.8474	5.5755	5.0916	4.6755	4.0013	3.4834	3.0764
7.8237	6.9740	6.2651	5.9542	5.6685	5.1624	4.7296	4.0333	3.5026	3.0882
8.0216	7.1196	6.3729	6.0472	5.7487	5.2223	4.7746	4.0591	3.5177	3.0971
8.2014	7.2497	6.4674	6.1280	5.8178	5.2732	4.8122	4.0799	3.5294	3.1039
8.3649	7.3658	6.5504	6.1982	5.8775	5.3162	4.8435	4.0967	3.5386	3.1090
8.5136	7.4694	6.6231	6.2593	5.9288	5.3527	4.8696	4.1103	3.5458	3.1129
8.6487	7.5620	6.6870	6.3125	5.9731	5.3837	4.8913	4.1212	3.5514	3.1158
8.7715	7.6446	6.7429	6.3587	6.0113	5.4099	4.9094	4.1300	3.5558	3.1180
8.8832	7.7184	6.7921	6.3988	6.0442	5.4321	4.9245	4.1371	3.5592	3.1197
8.9847	7.7843	6.8351	6.4338	6.0726	5.4509	4.9371	4.1428	3.5619	3.1210
9.0770	7.8431	6.8729	6.4641	6.0971	5.4669	4.9476	4.1474	3.5640	3.1220
9.4269	8.0552	7.0027	6.5660	6.1772	5.5168	4.9789	4.1601	3.5693	3.1242
9.7791	8.2438	7.1050	6.6418	6.2335	5.5482	4.9966	4.1659	3.5712	3.1250
9.9148	8.3045	7.1327	6.6605	6.2463	5.5541	4.9995	4.1666	3.5714	3.1250

Appendix C

NOTATION CONVERSION TABLE

Different authors and calculator manufacturers use different symbols to represent key financial variables, i.e., present value, future value, payment, interest rate and period. This table provides a quick comparison of symbols in several leading textbooks. Symbols used in *this* book are shown in parentheses in the first column.

	HP-10B	EL-733	BA II Plus	BH	BMM	RWJ Essent'ls	RWJ Fund'ls
Present Value (PV)	PV	PV	PV	PV	PV	PV	PV
Future Value (FV)	FV	FV	FV	FV	FV	FV	FV
Payment (PMT)	PMT	PMT	PMT	A	C	C	C
Interest Rate (i)	I/YR	i	I/Y	i	r	r	r
Maturity (n)	N	n	N	n	t	t	t

BH: Block, S. and G. Hirt. *Foundations of Financial Management, 9th Ed.*, (Burr Ridge, IL: Irwin/McGraw-Hill, 2000).

BMM: Brealey, R. A., S. C. Myers, and A. J. Marcus. *Fundamentals of Corporate Finance, 2nd Ed.,* (Burr Ridge, IL: Irwin/McGraw-Hill, 1999).

RWJ Essent'ls: Ross, S., R. Westerfield and B. Jordan. *Essentials of Corporate Finance, 2nd Ed.* (Burr Ridge, IL: Irwin/McGraw-Hill, 1999).

RWJ Fund'ls: Ross, S., R. Westerfield and B. Jordan. *Fundamentals of Corporate Finance, 5th Ed.,* (Burr Ridge, IL: Irwin/McGraw-Hill, 2000).